ONE INCREASING

ONE INCREASING PURPOSE

The Annals of an Investor

Lewis Whyte, CBE, FFA

HUTCHINSON BENHAM
London

Hutchinson Benham Ltd
An imprint of the Hutchinson Publishing Group
17–21 Conway Street, London W1P 6JD

Hutchinson Publishing Group (Australia) Pty Ltd
PO Box 496, 16–22 Church Street, Hawthorne, Melbourne,
Victoria 3122

Hutchinson Group (NZ) Ltd
32–34 View Road, PO Box 40-086, Glenfield, Auckland 10

Hutchinson Group (SA) Pty Ltd
PO Box 337, Bergvlei 2012, South Africa

First published 1984

Set in VIP Bembo by
D. P. Media Limited, Hitchin, Hertfordshire

Printed and bound in Great Britain by
Anchor Brendon Ltd, Tiptree, Essex

British Library Cataloguing in Publication Data
Whyte, Lewis
One increasing purpose
1. Investments – Great Britain
I. Title
332.6′092′4   HG5432
ISBN 0 09 155230 3

Contents

Foreword

After his distinguished career in finance and industry, private and public/governmental, Lewis Whyte could have sought an eminent name to commend his book. I am therefore flattered by his choice. I gladly accepted his invitation because I strongly encouraged him for various reasons to develop an early draft of several chapters.

Lewis Whyte writes with knowledge, flavoured by insights, in plain English. His integrity shines out, and illustrates my impression that standards of conduct are generally higher in private business than in public life because people who fall from grace are usually discovered sooner by the market than in politics. Also, people who work in private industry and rise to the top in achievement and responsibility write too rarely about their experiences. The result is that the repute of industry has suffered because the general public knows little of higher management, company direction, or the relationship between profit and risk-taking beyond the pages of the newspapers that dwell on the shortcomings rather than the achievements of industry. It has little impression of industry as much more challenging, stimulating and rewarding in confronting uncertainties in supply and demand than are the sheltered routines of 'public' services, and much more accountable than government to the real public it serves in competitive markets.

In an early response I urged Lewis Whyte to say more on his activities as an actuary and later as director and adviser in life assurance, private enterprise and nationalized industry. And this he has gone some way to do, with unique knowledge, authority and discretion, from his early days as an actuarial clerk at the Scottish Amicable Life Assurance Society in 1925 to his final task as a member of the National Freight Corporation, where after his retirement he observed with joy the launching in 1982 of an employee-owned private enterprise. He candidly reflects on his regrets and disappointments over fifty years, but ends with the conviction that private enterprise excels over 'public ownership' (incidentally, a misnomer, since the 'ownership' is nominal and the 'owners' cannot escape from inefficient management by selling their shares in the market). In his conclusion, Lewis Whyte confirms the expectations of liberal economists and the failure of 'public ownership'.

Not surprisingly, his paths crossed those of many of the *eminenti* in academia, industry and public life – from J. M. Keynes to Lord (Gordon) Richardson and from Lord Balogh to Lord Kearton and many more. He delivered a paper with Lord Piercy to the late Sir Ronald Edwards' celebrated seminar at the London School of Economics, but is one of the few authors of scholarly papers who have written their autobiographical histories in book length. His descriptions and recollections will whet the appetite of serious students of industry, who are happily increasing in number: Dr Leslie Hannah has recently been appointed Professor of Business History in the University of London at the London School of Economics; and Mr Neil MacKendrick has done pioneering work at Cambridge, not least by editing the Europa Library of Business Biographies, which he described (at an Institute of Economic Affairs seminar in

1. The Proceedings were published as *Prime Mover of Progress*, IEA, 1980s.

1979)[1] as 'a kind of "Life of the Entrepreneur" to match the nineteenth-century engineers'.

The entrepreneur is the catalyst of the progressive economy. In past centuries he was lauded as the 'merchant venturer'; for a hundred years he has been misunderstood, condemned and reviled. Yet the entrepreneurial *function* – delineated by Professor Israel Kirzner as the capacity to detect wants and the alertness to mobilize labour and capital to satisfy them – has to be performed in every economic system from capitalism to communism. The question is in which system it is more likely to emerge and to benefit the populace with imagination, initiative, capacity to assess and run risks. There can be little doubt that the free market offers the best environment.

Yet the activities, successes and failures of entrepreneurs are too little understood. If entrepreneurs will not or cannot go even as far as Lewis Whyte in writing their reflections, it will fall to scholars to repair the gap. And insofar as developments are not recorded in writing, but are increasingly conducted by telephone and other mechanized marvels, they can be preserved by supplementing documented history with recollections (accounts) recalled by the people who created them. Oral history[2] will have to be used increasingly: the recollections in tranquillity years after the event can be subjective and subconsciously used to disguise disagreeable events, but documented history, as with minutes of company directors' (or Cabinet ministers') meetings, can be even more defective since it is written at the time when it can influence events by omission and emphasis.

Lewis Whyte's reflections emphasize the lessons of experience. He remarks of a mutual life assurance office that it had 'no shareholders urging growth, increased profits,

2. The subject is discussed in *By Word of Mouth*, Methuen, 1983, by Dr Joanna Pappworth and Dr Anthony Seldon.

and higher dividends. It must have been a cosy and un-worrying existence with the minimum of tensions.' In an open society people can come together to organize activities either 'communally' without money passing, or for 'profit' made in trade. But the 'non-profit' organization is not necessarily superior to the profit-motivated. Men moved by a sense of mission may do outstanding work, but they generally lack the sense of urgency generated by competition that can be met only by cutting out waste and covering costs. This is a lesson Lewis Whyte confirms from his experience in both non-profit and profit-oriented undertakings.

His streak of entrepreneurship is best illustrated by his decision to 'sack himself' from the board of Equity and Law when he found after more than ten years that life assurance alone did not fulfil his aspirations or satisfy his wider interests. 'So I cut the painter and created a vacuum which sooner or later I would have to fill myself.' It was not long before he was recommended for directorial posts in several industries, including motors (AEC), finance of industry (ICFC), unit trusts (Save and Prosper), Kuwait Investment, Broadstone Investment, and, not least, again insurance (London and Manchester Assurance), where he followed Lord Grantchester as chairman. These activities led to others with increasing responsibility.

It is intriguing to read that this man of modest demeanour was also a director of ACV, the National Coal Board (where Lord Robens encouraged his wish to visit a good pit but discouraged him from a poor pit, and where he declined to serve a second term), chairman of the Transport Holding Company (in which he presided over the denationalization of Thomas Cook), member of the National Freight Corporation, and a deputy chairman of British Leyland.

Lewis Whyte was the author of one of the official text-books in 1949/50 for the students of the Institute and the Faculty of Actuaries, entitled *Principles of Finance and*

10

Investment (2 vols.). It was based almost entirely on theory. His new book is based on fifty years of practical experience and will make rewarding reading for many in the financial professions.

Although written in a low key, the book touches on many disputatious aspects of current – and coming – public policy on the control of industry. I could have wished for even more discussion and analysis, but I hope his book encourages other industrial leaders to do at least as much, if not more, for the scholarly student of industry, for the repute of private enterprise, and to correct the popularizers, the ideologically hostile academics, the newspaper over-simplifiers.

The merchant venturer is still essential in British industry. The conditions in which he can best emerge could increasingly be revealed in accounts by men and women with personal experience of challenges and their successes or failures in overcoming them. Lewis Whyte was more than a Scottish actuary. Professor F. A. Hayek has argued that in a state economy the worst often rise to the top. This book will tell us more not only of the author and his work but also of the economic system that enables the best to rise to the top.

Arthur Seldon
of the Institute of Economic Affairs
September 1983

11

Introduction

Yet I doubt not thro' the ages one increasing purpose runs,
And the thoughts of men are widen'd with the process of the suns.

from 'Locksley Hall' by Alfred, Lord Tennyson

The title of this book was prompted by one of the few long poems that I was made to learn by heart at school, and to this day there are many lines I still remember. I recollect being moved by the superb words of the rhyming couplets and by the resilient optimism of the narrator, who believed that, in spite of bitter disappointments and frustration, all in the end would be well.

My business life fell into four separate parts: life assurance and the actuarial profession; investment; the motor industry; and involvement with nationalized industries. Some overlapped; but I shall deal with each in turn.

Among the several reasons for writing this book is the realization that in my student days all the textbooks were based solely on theory. I can recall no writing which explained how problems, whether in life assurance or investment, were solved in practice. Having spent over forty years in life assurance with its associated investment problems, and having worked for three life assurance companies which in different ways had been in acute financial difficulties, I feel that I have acquired the practical experience to fill this particular vacuum.

Another reason is to acknowledge the debt of gratitude I owe to the many who have helped me in my career. Their names will appear in the course of the narrative. Here, however, I would like to thank the kind friends who have helped in the preparation of this book. First, Arthur Seldon, of the Institute of Economic Affairs, who read some of the earlier drafts and encouraged me to complete the task and in addition gave much valuable advice. My grateful thanks are due also to the four who checked the facts, though not the opinions, of the main chapters. They are: David Jubb, chief executive of London and Manchester Assurance Company, the chapter on 'Life Assurance'; Freddie Bodem of Henderson Crosthwaite & Co, stockbrokers, 'Investment'; Lord Black, former chairman of Leyland Motor Corporation, 'The Motor Industry'; and John Peyton (now Lord Peyton), former Minister of Transport, 'The Public Sector'. In addition to verifying the facts, all gave me helpful comments and advice.

I am also very grateful to Elizabeth Twiston-Davies, who typed the manuscript and kept a watchful eye on spelling and syntax.

One final caveat; several of the thoughts in the narrative impinge on current affairs, and as a few months may elapse between going to press and publication some of them will probably have been overtaken by subsequent events. If any such inconsistencies should emerge I hope the reader will understand.

CHAPTER 1
Early Beginnings

I was born in 1906 in Helensburgh, a pleasant town on the north bank of the River Clyde, about twenty-five miles west of Glasgow. My father was Scottish, an architect, and my mother was American, born in Detroit. Her father was employed in the Singer Sewing Machine Company in America, and when the large factory was opened in Scotland near the end of the century, he and many other Americans came to work and live nearby. The new factory near Clydebank – alas, now closed – was about halfway between Glasgow and Helensburgh, and most of the Americans settled in Helensburgh and established a lively American community there.

One annual event was the 'American Picnic', presumably on 4 July. Horse-drawn coaches were hired for the twenty or so families, and we were driven to a shore of Loch Lomond to picnic and play games, but seldom, if ever, to bathe in the cold waters. This American environment did much in later years to lessen the strangeness I might otherwise have felt during business trips to the United States and Canada.

My father spent most of his working life with John Brown & Co. Ltd, shipbuilders of Clydebank, his work being the designing and decorating of the interiors of ocean liners. Many famous ships were built by John Brown's, the shipping lines including the Blue Star, New Zealand Shipping, Orient Line and Cunard: the best known of all the ships were the two Queens.

When the *Queen Mary* was being built, and before the naming, she was designated No. 534. In the early 1930s, when the world slump was at its nadir, the Cunard Steamship Company ran out of money and work was suspended for about two years: the most agonizing industrial event I have ever witnessed. Later, with the help of government guarantees and finance, work was resumed: surely one of the most beneficial commercial interventions ever made by government.

I was told a tale about the name which sounds plausible, though I cannot be certain of its authenticity. All Cunard liners then had names ending in '—*ia*': *Aquitania*, *Mauretania*, *Berengaria*, etc., and a logical choice would have been *Victoria* for the great new No. 534. The chairman of Cunard was alleged to have approached the sovereign, King George V, and in extravagant language asked permission to name the ship after 'England's greatest queen', whereupon the King is believed to have replied: 'My wife would be delighted.' The lesson to be learned, if there is one, is: 'Don't beat about the bush; go straight to the point!'

I used to see these big ocean liners at all stages: on the stocks when they were being built; occasionally when they were launched; sometimes on a private visit, shortly before the maiden voyage; and almost every week I had a sight of them on the Clyde at the 'tail of the bank', when they called on their way from Liverpool to New York or Montreal. I thought then that they were the most beautiful man-made creations ever built, and I still think so. When in 1978 I met Nigel Broackes, the chairman of Trafalgar Investments, the owners of Cunard Steamship, we discussed the likely life of the present flagship, *Queen Elizabeth 2*, which might be thirty or forty years; but he added the comment that it would never be replaced. I immediately assumed the reason would be the prohibitive cost; but I was told that the real reason was that there was no longer any shipyard in the United Kingdom that knew how to build large passenger liners. *Sic transit gloria mundi.*

Among my earliest recollections is of attending my kindergarten school in Helensburgh: about twenty boys, between the ages of six and eight, under the sole care of Miss Johnston in her own home. We sat round a large, oval table. There was no class tuition as such. Miss Johnston sat beside each pupil in turn and gave him individual attention. She was kindly, yet a firm believer in discipline. All who remember her would agree that she gave the best grounding possible in 'the three Rs', and she took a keen personal interest in all her pupils until she died.

In due course I moved to the local school, Larchfield, where I remained throughout the First World War. The staff were accordingly female or C3 males: yet I recollect that the standard of education was excellent. About one-tenth of the pupils were boarders; the rest were day-boys. It was an unusual school, in that the great majority of boys were of preparatory school age, up to ages fourteen or fifteen, while a dozen or so were aged eighteen or just under. It was not a good arrangement. Just imagine playing rugby football in those circumstances – especially when some of the masters joined in as well! Before I left, orthodoxy prevailed and the school became preparatory only.

Helensburgh was in many ways a pleasant town to grow up in, though the climate is enervating. One of its residents, the author Neil Munro, described the town's main occupation as 'travelling to Glasgow', which was only too true. Among its famous citizens were Andrew Bonar Law and John Logie Baird, the inventor of television and of radar. The travellers were divided into two groups: the 'strivers', who took the early morning train; and the 'thrivers', who took the later one. The town was laid out on the grid system, and in the early days of motoring, before traffic lights had been invented, it was a highly dangerous town for traffic. The only street then enjoying the right of way was the hilly Colquhoun Street, in winter reserved solely for tobogganing.

Most of the houses had beautiful, well-kept gardens, tended by part-time or full-time gardeners. Teenagers had a full and happy social life. Every winter there were numerous dances, held in private houses and, occasionally, in the large local 'Victoria Halls'.

When the time came for me to leave Larchfield my parents decided to send me to Trinity College, Glenalmond. They were told I might have a reasonable chance of winning a scholarship. I duly sat for the common entrance examination, supervised by the headmaster at Larchfield. The only thing I remember was having to draw an opened umbrella, which, if one thinks about it, is very difficult to draw in proper perspective. After an interview with the Warden of Glenalmond at Perth and a further Latin test, I was awarded a scholarship of £30 per annum, which in those days was a useful saving to my father.

I have never subscribed to the dictum that 'Schooldays are the happiest days of your life.' There were pleasures: Glenalmond is in the heart of Perthshire, remote from any town; the countryside is beautiful, and the summer terms were enjoyable. We bathed in the River Almond every afternoon; and most Saturdays, when there were no cricket matches, we could roam far and wide with a picnic lunch. But the two winter terms could be very grim indeed. A cold bath had to be taken every morning, however low the temperature, and quite often in midwinter we would find, on awakening, thick ice in our washbasins.

Of course, one goes to school to be educated, and I believe the education at Glenalmond was very good. This was due more to the excellence of most of the masters than to the curriculum. I remember one master in particular who had the art of teaching the boys to teach themselves, and not to rely on learning by rote – an invaluable lesson when I came to earn my living. When I had to think about choosing a career, I was told that mathematics was my best subject. My father held the view that chartered accountancy might become an overcrowded profession, but he was in touch with a few actuaries who told him a little of what was involved and I was guided towards that idea. The school was most cooperative, and it was arranged that during my last term I should do nothing except advanced mathematics. The dedicated maths master probably learned more than I did. It certainly initiated him for the first time into the mysteries of the differential calculus.

I was glad to leave school, yet if I had to live that part of my life all over again I would rather go to Glenalmond than to any other school I could imagine. There was never any question of my going to a university. In those days, it would not have helped much in my actuarial training and would probably have delayed the time when I could qualify. Family finances were such that the sooner I earned my living, the better.

CHAPTER 2
Life Assurance

Actuarial Training with the Scottish Amicable Life Assurance Society, 1925–30

I left school at the end of the Easter term 1925, and within a few days I sat Part 1 of the examinations of the Faculty of Actuaries in Scotland. At the beginning of May I joined the staff of the Scottish Amicable Life Assurance Society in Glasgow, on the lowest rung of the ladder. The examination was held in a large and austere hall of Edinburgh University and I was, understandably, nervous and apprehensive. The papers were very difficult – much more so than I had expected – but I answered most of the questions somehow and left with a faint hope of success. I recollect that one of my fellow-students seemed determined to demonstrate his disgust with the very stiff papers. At about half-time he noisily folded his papers, took out his pipe and lit it. He was firmly reprimanded.

When the results came out, about a month later, only six candidates out of fifty-six for Part 1 had passed. I was not one of the six. I learned later that my marks were 22 per cent against a pass-mark of 55 per cent. Although I was distressed and deeply shocked, this dismal failure was the best thing that could have happened to me. It was my first lesson that a dose of adversity, though painful at the time, can be wonderfully beneficial in time to come. I realized that these examinations were unlike anything I had had to cope with at school, and that a very determined effort would be necessary. I did not fail again, and I qualified in 1929, learning that my marks in the final were 55.15 per cent – a close shave!

The only oral tuition classes were at the headquarters of the Faculty of Actuaries in Edinburgh, and they were not feasible for anyone studying and working in Glasgow. So I enrolled in a correspondence tuition course with the excellent Mr P. M. Marples of Birmingham. During the study times I received weekly tuition papers with courses of reading and weekly or fortnightly tests, which were always returned within a few days, duly marked, with helpful marginal notes. The disadvantages of tuition by correspondence are obvious: the lack of ready personal contact with the tutor, and the absence of fraternal contact with one's fellow-students. But there were advantages as well, for one was not a slave to a fixed timetable. I owed much to Mr Marples, though regrettably it was not until after I had qualified that I met him in person and was able to thank him properly.

Actuarial examinations require not only a profound knowledge of all matters in the syllabus but also, and in a unique way, the ability to perform well in the examination room. Questions were often set on problems which had never been rehearsed, and which were quite new to the student. Brilliant ability in examinations without adequate knowledge could never be enough, but excellent knowledge without the examination-room technique could bring bitter disappointment.

I duly received my certificate stating that I was qualified 'as to his knowledge of the Doctrine of Probabilities and the Theory and Practice of Life Assurance'. It often occurred to me afterwards that it seemed strange that this certificate could have been issued without my ever having been summoned to appear in person before the board of examiners.

Everything depended on the marks obtained in the written examination. A better system might have been a lower pass-mark, but the result dependent upon performing satisfactorily also at an interview.

Those four years were the hardest and least enjoyable of my business life. I soon settled into a yearly routine. The examinations were normally held in May, and I did not study in the early summer months. The grind started in September. There was a full Faculty library in Glasgow, so I never lacked for reading material. I lived in Helensburgh and commuted by train every day to Glasgow. The journey was about three-quarters of an hour each way, and I always studied in the train. A seat was always available, and the yearly season ticket was £18. Any reading of newspapers was very cursory. When I got home I studied all evening, with time off only for the evening meal. I usually stopped at about 10.30 p.m., went for a walk, and then to bed. I never 'burned the midnight oil'. During the day, in the office, frequent intervals with nothing to do gave me further opportunities to study. I usually worked in the office on Saturday mornings, and I had a rest on Saturday afternoons and all of Sunday.

Shortly before the examinations the office gave the students about four afternoons off for study. I usually used them for fresh air and exercise, rather than for extra study. I had soon learned that a fresh mind and a healthy body were essential – so much so that I stopped all study about three days before the examination, though I refreshed myself by looking through my notes in the train on the mornings of the examinations themselves. This warming-up helped the mental engine to tick over, and not have to start 'cold', from scratch, in the examination room.

The syllabus and examinations were, of course, designed for the practical work of a qualified actuary, but in a much wider sense they proved to be a valuable training for many other walks of life. The study of probability helps one to 'calculate the odds', and the statistical training helps one to marshal the relevant facts. Thus, if in any problem one can estimate the reward if things went right and the penalty if they went wrong, and at the same time assess the probability of either happening, then one has the best available instrument for forming a good judgement. These criteria could, for example, be used in proposals for exploration and development in the case of North Sea oil, and almost without exception in investment problems.

The Scottish Amicable was, in 1925, just about to celebrate its first centenary. By the standards of the time it was a medium-sized mutual life office, with funds of about £10 million and new sums assured at about £1 million per annum. Of its staff of a few hundred, about one hundred worked at the head office in Glasgow, so all faces there were soon familiar. The board consisted of non-executive directors, in the main Glasgow businessmen, together with the general manager, the chairman rotating every year or two. Although I was much too junior ever to attend a board meeting, I imagined that their main functions were to appoint the senior officials and to deliberate on investment matters. New appointments to the board were made by the board and ratified by the annual meeting of policy-holders, which was a mere formality.

The general manager, William Hutton, was my first encounter with 'supreme authority'. I was never formally introduced; I was merely told, 'As soon as you see him you will recognize him as "the Chief".' I did. He was my first business hero: majestic, shrewd, austere, yet with a kindly twinkle in his eye. Although a stern and demanding boss, he was especially kind to juniors. He was usually one of the first to congratulate me on my examination passes, and he went to great trouble to find me a new post when I left the society.

There were no shareholders urging growth, increased profits and higher dividends. It must have been a cosy and

23

unworrying existence with the minimum of tension. The motivation came primarily from the excellence of the senior officials, nearly all of whom were actuaries. The top priority was the maintenance of a high and competitive level of reversionary bonus, valuations taking place quinquennially. The urge for growth and expansion came more from the sum of individual efforts than from a corporate drive. Everyone in the new business field, whether branch manager or inspector of agents, was aware that his personal prospects depended upon his own individual performance, and this was a very effective stimulus, corporate as well as personal.

Investment of the society's funds must have been relatively uncomplicated by modern standards. The cult of the equity was in its pre-natal state, and the number of industrial equities in the society's portfolio could then be numbered on the fingers on one hand. Investment was mainly confined to fixed-interest securities of all kinds and to preference stocks and shares. Foreign government stocks played a prominent part, and default was very rare. Great Britain had just returned to the gold standard, and inflation was a word to be found only in economic textbooks. Deflation was then the enemy.

When I started, as the most junior clerk, my main duties were to read all the letters to see that the right enclosures were in fact enclosed, to copy them on a Roneo machine for filing the next day, and to address and stamp all the envelopes. I also acted as messenger for many miscellaneous jobs.

Although premiums and claims were normally paid by cheque, salaries in those days were always paid in cash. Once a month my immediate colleague and I were handed a cheque by the cashier and told to cash it at the local bank in specified denominations of notes and coin. These were put into envelopes by the cashier and distributed among the management and staff. (My own monthly envelope in my

24

first year contained £3.6s.8d., of which £1 was surrendered to the family housekeeping budget.) Soon afterwards the general manager's buzzer would sound and I was instructed to put the greater part of his own monthly cash into his bank in Glasgow. I thought at the time that all this was rather a silly arrangement. Little was known then of the mysteries of 'time-and-motion' study.

Another example of the distrust of credit in those days was the weekly system of getting the policies stamped at the local office of the Inland Revenue. I was handed the policies with the appropriate cheque, but before the Inland Revenue would accept it I had to go to the bank to get it guaranteed. This procedure was probably the relic of something initiated in the previous century. It is an interesting reflection on which was the more creditworthy: the bank or the assurance society.

After a year or so at the post desk, I was moved to the actuarial department, where I learned how to calculate surrender values, paid-up values, alteration to policy terms, and so on. It was useful experience for my examinations, but I soon became aware that predetermined formulae precluded any scope for judgement, and this did much to disenchant me with routine actuarial work. Then, a few months later, I learned by chance that a vacancy was about to occur in the investment department, so I called on the sole clerk to enquire about his successor. He told me that I had been considered, but that the management thought I would not welcome a further change so soon. Scenting the prospect of promotion, rather than feeling any great desire to be concerned with investments, I put myself forward, and to my delight was given the job.

The investment organization then consisted of the general manager, the assistant manager (later the investment manager) and one clerk – myself. It was a unique experience for me, and it undoubtedly sowed the seeds of the interest and fascination investment has held for me ever since.

I had to calculate the yields on all purchases and sales, and occasionally prepare a synopsis for the board. I kept the investment portfolio up to date, and did the yearly valuation. Certificates were kept by me under lock and key for examination by the auditors. For all this responsibility I was paid £150 per year; but the education was priceless.

The telephone in the department was seldom used except for local calls, and on the management floor there was only one telephone available. All communication with London was done by letter or telegram, and many a time I had to seek my boss in another part of Glasgow to deliver an urgent message and despatch a reply.

When I qualified as an actuary in 1929, I had to think about my future. I was anxious to get away from the west of Scotland. I had found the climate there far from invigorating. I had no longing to seek my fortune in Edinburgh, which was the chief centre of life assurance in Scotland; I wanted to see something of the wider world. Having learned of the prestige and expansion of the Canadian life companies, I wrote to several, seeking interviews in their British offices. But the Wall Street crash was giving way to the great depression of the early 1930s, and there seemed to be a great reluctance to make new recruits. So I sought a job in the investment world in London, hoping for an opening in one of the merchant banks. The times were far from propitious, but with the help of many introductions by the management of the Scottish Amicable I was offered and accepted a post with Buckmaster and Moore, stockbrokers, in London, where I stayed for ten years.

Before I joined the firm I was involved in a strange hiatus. During my visits to London in search of work I received much kind help from Francis Fenton, London secretary of the Scottish Amicable. When he heard that I had been offered a post with Buckmaster & Moore he warned me of a worrying event. The firm had recently issued to its clients a circular decrying most British investments and praising most American ones. This received adverse comment in the House of Commons, and Fenton thought that patriotic reaction in the City and country might do the firm serious harm. As I was keen to get established in London, I ignored the warning. In the event, the firm's advice proved not to be good, for in the ensuing three years, while most British stocks fell heavily, the fall in America was even greater.

During my time with Buckmaster & Moore, I was much under the influence of the senior active partner, Ian Macpherson, a determined Scotsman who had started his business career as a barrister. He was a skilled stockbroker with a gift of persuasive exposition, and he taught me much of the art of investment, for which I have always been grateful.

One of my best friends in the firm was Denis Scott, who was manoeuvred into premature resignation – and I deeply regret that I did not defend him more vehemently. However, when he returned to business after the war he did much better than he would probably have done had he remained in the firm. As a director of Broadstone Investment Trust he was responsible for my joining that board, and as a director of Save and Prosper Group he was a constant help and supporter of my activities there. Sadly, his promising career was cut short by his untimely death in the prime of life.

By the spring of 1939 I had decided that it was time for me to leave stockbroking and return to life assurance. I had to give a year's notice, and did so in April, but I could not begin to seek new work until the year's notice was nearly up. When war was declared John Maynard Keynes, whom I had got to know well, recommended me for the Ministry of Economic Warfare. When he wrote to say there was nothing doing there, he made the comment that the authorities had been 'comatose'. When I told him later that I had been appointed investment manager of Equity and Law

Life Assurance Society, he wrote a charming letter of good wishes hoping that I would soon develop a 'technique of getting your own way without your board knowing too much about it'. Sadly, I lost touch with him and was never challenged on whether I had been able to follow his advice.

Equity and Law Life Assurance Society, 1940–53

In 1939 I was appointed investment manager of the Equity and Law Life Assurance Society, to start at the end of April 1940. The Equity and Law was in several ways unique. Its constitution then stipulated that no one was eligible to be a director unless he was connected with the legal profession: in practice, this meant he had to be a solicitor or a barrister. The share capital, all ordinary, was in the form of £20 shares, £1 paid up, but with unlimited liability. In the immediate pre-war period a vast expansion of new business had taken place through the encouragement of single premiums and the lending of a high proportion of its funds on mortgages, repayable by life assurance policies lodged as collateral security.

The nervous financial background due to the threat of war was soon undermining the security of many of the society's mortgages, and the financial position of the society at the outbreak of war was precarious. My responsibilities as investment manager covered all the assets, including property and mortgages, about which I knew very little, as well as the Stock Exchange investments, where I was on more familiar ground. I soon learned that the only effective way of assessing and safeguarding mortgages was to make contact with the borrowers and to inspect the property or business in mortgage.

Properties directly owned as an investment did not present problems for me, as there was always at hand the opinion of the society's experienced valuer and surveyor. Among the miscellaneous businesses held in mortgage which I visited were several film studios, hotels in Bournemouth, a coal-mine and brickworks in the Midlands, farm estates in the north of Scotland and in Yorkshire, a confectionery business in Hertfordshire, a golf course in the Home Counties, a brewery in Lancashire and a large drapery store in Dublin. This last establishment involved me in an interesting adventure. The society had lent on mortgage £200,000. For various reasons it could not obtain, as collateral, the customary life assurance on the managing director, but was offered and accepted policies for £25,000 each on eight Roman Catholic priests – who, I think, had nothing to do with the fortunes of the store. In 1940 the store was doing badly, the mortgage went into default and a receiver was appointed. I was sent over to Dublin to investigate and to do the best I could. I flew from Manchester in a tiny civilian aeroplane: halfway across the Irish Sea it was diverted back to Liverpool owing to the proximity of German aircraft. Eventually I arrived in Dublin and negotiated with the interested parties well into the small hours of the morning. The business was sold by the receiver to an astute business rival for a sum little more than the amount of the mortgage plus arrears. The shareholders then used the tiny excess to bring an action against the receiver on the grounds of selling at an undervalue.

The case came for hearing at the Four Courts in Dublin in the following spring, and I was summoned to appear as a material witness. It lasted several days and the judge – a well-known Sinn Feiner and one of the signatories of the Anglo-Irish treaty – gave judgement for the receiver, the appointee of an English assurance company. I remember being moved by the complete impartiality of the judgement. The new owner made a great success of the business and in due course the loan was repaid in full. The eight policies were all surrendered by agreement after the new owner and mortgagee had satisfied himself that all of the priests appeared to be in good health.

One of the longest journeys I took was in 1941 to the north of Scotland to visit a laird in the 'Black Isle', north of Inverness, where we had lent money on security of his castle and estate, covering some of the most fertile land in the kingdom. I took the night sleeper from Euston, and when dawn broke in Speyside I looked out of the window to see a perfect sunrise beyond the Cairngorms, which, though it was midsummer, were still covered with snow. At Inverness I had to go through a security barrier into a restricted area, and when the officer examined my pass and the reasons for it he said that he hoped I would give a good report, as the laird in question was a close friend of his – a nice human touch! I stayed in a hotel in Dingwall, one of the so-called 'Carlisle Experiment', which had inaugurated soon after 1918 several hotels and pubs to be owned by the state, and prompted, I believe, by temperance people who thought the idea would discourage excessive drinking. Although it is against my political philosophy to say so, I admit it was one of the best hotels of its grade I have ever stayed in. Any wartime rationing of food and drink was notable by its absence.

On my return south I diverted to visit a similar estate in north Yorkshire. In both cases I was received with courtesy and kindly hospitality. These visits did much to confirm my view that more can often be done by personal contact than by dozens of letters, even though the parties may be on different sides of the fence. And when letters have subsequently to be written, it is always an advantage for the correspondents to know each other.

The film studios in the mortgage portfolio presented less trouble than might have been expected. There was then a good demand for British films. Some studios were requisitioned for storage of food and materials.

There were no established rules about how to deal with mortgages in default, or likely to default. It was usually a common-sense approach to find out what the borrower could pay, and to refrain from taking action as long as such payments on account were duly made. One large commitment was mortgages on houses in Palestine with life policies as collateral security. They were all handled by an able agent on the spot, and although they caused much anxiety I believe that at the end of the day hardly a penny was lost.

In the latter part of 1940 the society's position was critical, and well before 31 December, the normal end of its financial year, the management (which was effectively Bob Kirton, general manager, Trevor Haynes, actuary, and myself) decided on a valuation of the assets and a rough estimate of the liabilities. I do not remember the precise outcome, but the margin on the right side was very small indeed, and the room for manoeuvre was tightly restricted. Largely as a consequence of this investigation the society's constitution was altered to allow a proportion of non-legal directors, and some new directors were co-opted with the help and advice of the governor of the Bank of England.

At this time Sir Geoffrey Ellis, Bt., MP, took over as chairman, and I worked happily under him until he retired seven years later. I owe much to his influence. He was a barrister, banker and industrialist, as well as a politician. When I went to him with an investment proposal, and he agreed, I had instinctive confidence that we were right. If he disagreed, he never tried openly to persuade me to his point of view but, by skilful examination and cross-examination, he tried to lead me to his way of thinking as if it were my own, and this often worked. If I could not be persuaded, he would usually agree – but I was under notice to re-examine my arguments.

When I thanked him on his retirement I added that working for him had been great 'fun', then apologized for using a flippant word. He immediately answered that it was certainly the right word, adding, 'if you don't have fun in your work, you can never give your best.'

31

The quite understandable thinking in 1940–41 was that there could be no bonus on with-profit policies and no dividend. Having learned during my years with the Stock Exchange how vital was the factor of confidence, and foreseeing the havoc which would come to the £20 shares, £1 paid, with unlimited liability, if confidence were lost, I pleaded strongly for the payment of some token dividend. The advice was taken, and for the year 1940 a nominal dividend of one shilling per share was declared, which, if I remember correctly, cost the society £10,000 gross – not an expensive insurance premium against probable disaster.

As the war took a turn for the better after the Battle of Britain and the battles in the western desert, so the investment markets improved and the fear of financial crisis in the society receded. From the beginning of 1941 onwards, there was a steady and sustained improvement in its finances, but the restoration of confidence among the insuring public and its advisers was a slow and uphill task. New business fell to a trickle and in one of the mid-war years new sums assured did not reach even the £1 million mark, against about £1,000 million at the time of writing. Confidence is a very tender plant. It can wither quickly but may take many long years to recover.

Like most insurance offices in wartime, the Equity and Law had a country office – an old mansion near Kings Langley, Herts. Its head office in Lincoln's Inn Fields was requisitioned and occupied by the Royal Canadian Air Force. A small London presence was found in the Strand. In spite of these difficulties the administration worked smoothly and efficiently.

While my work with Equity and Law was almost entirely concerned with Stock Exchange investments and the supervision of mortgages, there was one noteworthy involvement with industrial development shortly after the end of the war which took up much of my time and caused not a little anxiety. It came about in this way. One of the large mortgages made before the war was on the security of film studios at Shepperton under the control of an ebullient Scotsman, Norman Loudon. Few films were made there during the war, but income was supplemented by leasing part of the premises to government agencies for storage. Loudon then conceived and carried out the ingenious idea of fabricating dummy cities and siting them on green fields near big cities, for example in Richmond Park. When air-raids started the dummies were set on fire to act as decoys.

With his experience of studio work, Loudon had become familiar with one of the main raw materials of film studios – gypsum plaster. Soon after the war ended, and when rebuilding of houses, schools and hospitals became an urgent priority, he invented and patented a type of load-bearing wall panel. This consisted of two smooth faces of plaster bonded together with hessian, impregnated with plaster in the shape of a honeycomb, the finished panel measuring about 4 feet by 3 feet. It was easy to make with unskilled labour. Wet plaster was poured into two metal trays. The hessian scrim was placed on a matrix of honeycomb design, the liquid plaster applied with a brush, and the product sawn into appropriate sizes with a band-saw. The panel was fire-resistant.

Loudon formed a company named Bellrock Gypsum Industries Ltd, which secured its supply of gypsum by acquiring the mineral rights of a gypsum deposit at Staunton, Nottinghamshire. A calcining plant was erected at the site, where raw gypsum was extracted and crushed, the water extracted, and the gypsum made into fine powder, like cement. When water was added the product could be moulded, and when dry would set into the required shape.

At the same time, with the help of friends in Jamaica, Loudon formed another company, Bellrock Caribbean, to take over and operate a vast deposit of gypsum in a hill a few miles from Kingston.

Loudon, of course, needed finance, and he came to

Equity and Law for this purpose. He wanted a loan of about £250,000 to Bellrock Gypsum Industries with collateral security of a large shareholding in Bellrock Caribbean; a small interest in the equity of both companies would be available. With his background in the film industry, Loudon lost no opportunity to present his proposals in the most optimistic vein, and I was convinced by much of his enthusiasm. I accordingly recommended the investment to the board and after much discussion and with considerable doubt the commitment was agreed. With Loudon's wish, and because of the board's doubts I was put on the boards of both Bellrock companies and accepted the positions with hope and a heavy weight of responsibility.

I then set to work to learn about his new venture. The mining of the raw gypsum at Staunton presented no problems. The over-burden of earth was shallow, and when removed exposed a bed of gypsum rock which was removed by mechanical shovels. The calcining plant had been constructed under the supervision of a former executive of the British Plaster Board Company. The plants where the Bellrock panels were fabricated were at Egham, near Loudon's home, and in Scotland, near the port of Grangemouth. The critical problem was to get customers. A moderate demand came from builders for use in building schools where speed and cheapness were essential and perfection of finish not so important. It soon became evident that the most intractable problem with these novel panels, which by themselves formed excellent parts of prefabricated walls, was that they proved very difficult to join together without disclosing a visible joint.

In total, sales were disappointing and no hopeful profits were made. Thus the security of the Equity and Law's loan would have to rely mainly on the success of the Jamaican company. I visited the operations in Jamaica on three occasions and considered myself fortunate in being able to visit this charming island, usually in the middle of an English winter. The first visit was in the nature of reconnaissance. The gypsum find was clearly visible: a cliff-face with a height of well over 100 feet of beautifully white mineral, extending presumably far into a hillside, a few miles west of Kingston. At the top of the cliff, Jamaican workers drove holes into the rock, by hand, with steel shafts. Explosives were then used to break off pieces of rock which tumbled to the ground at the base of the cliff. These were then conveyed by truck to the harbour, about a mile away, where a specially constructed loading tower conveyed the pieces of gypsum rock straight into the hold of the ship. A year or so after my first visit, this loading tower was torn down and thrown into the sea by an exceptionally vicious hurricane; but it was adequately insured and was restored to full working order a few months later.

The Bellrock panel was never used to any great extent in Jamaica, owing to its vulnerability to a local pest – the termite. Thus Bellrock Caribbean would have to depend entirely on the sale of raw gypsum, and soon a modest demand emerged. Sales of a few thousand tons each were made to the local cement company, to a few islands in the Caribbean and to Central and South America. The big prize was to break into the North American market. The resident managing director in Jamaica, Alastair Fraser, worked hard and got an order for an experimental shipment to the largest American gypsum company, US Gypsum. They were so pleased with the pure quality of the product that they began to think seriously of an outright purchase of the deposit.

In the meantime, Bellrock Caribbean had to explore every practicable means of mining and transporting substantial tonnage at an economical cost. The idea was mooted that the Colonial Development Corporation might provide cheap finance to construct an aerial ropeway for bringing large quantities from the rock face down to the loading tower at the harbour. My second visit was largely concerned with preparing a submission to the CDC and the opportunity was taken to inspect a similar type of aerial ropeway installed by an American aluminium company to shift bauxite from hills on the north coast of the island.

It is a sad commentary that Britain missed out in developing the vast quantities of bauxite on the island, still then a Crown Colony. The local legend is that a farmer was so dissatisfied with his crops that he sent a sample of his soil to be tested at a local research station. The reply came back: 'There is nothing wrong with your soil except that it is lousy with bauxite.' Evidently, this farmer was able to interest American companies more convincingly than the British ones.

Before the idea of the aerial ropeway got very far, Fraser had got US Gypsum seriously interested in an outright purchase, and before long an offer of $1 million was made. Loudon was a skilled and fearless negotiator, and replied that the price was $2 million (several times the original cost), 'Not a dollar less, take it or leave it.' After many weeks of to-ing and fro-ing, in which I remained an interested and anxious observer, the price of $2 million was agreed, subject to geological survey and proving.

My last journey to Jamaica was unforgettable. On a cold February morning I got on to the aeroplane at Heathrow bound for Bermuda, Bahamas and Jamaica via Gander, Newfoundland. The aeroplane was a heavy double-decker stratocruiser with four propellers – not a jet. The captain opened the proceedings by announcing that we would make an 'operational' stop at Keflavik, Iceland. When we crossed over the Solway Firth the sun was shining without a cloud in the sky, and Scotland was covered in snow from coast to coast. We flew up the west coast, and I could easily recognize the lochs and islands I knew so well. It was a lovely sight. We swung westwards over the Hebrides and landed in Iceland, which looked from the air like an imaginary moonscape. Our flight to Gander, was uneventful, but we passed within sight of 'Greenland's Icy Mountains'.

Instead of the expected half-hour stopover at Gander we were told we would have to stay the night, as winds at Bermuda were too strong. The dormitory facilities were adequate, though not luxurious, and soon after breakfast we were ready to take off. The snow was about 3 feet deep, but the runway was well swept. Because of the cold the engines were reluctant to start, and when we did take off we immediately met an intense snowstorm. Turbulence was severe, and for most of the journey to Bermuda even the wing-tips were invisible because of the density of snow. Reading was impossible and no refreshments – not even a cup of coffee – could be served. It was boring, rather than frightening. About halfway, the weather suddenly changed. The snow ceased and the sun came out; but before anyone could shout for joy the plane fell several hundred feet in a few seconds, and most of the hand-luggage fell off the racks. Very soon we were back in the blinding snow: we had passed through the eye of the hurricane. After brief stops at Bermuda and Nassau we arrived at Jamaica, hours late, to be met by anxious friends who had wearily waited at the airport.

On this final trip I was able to see US Gypsum and its geologists at work. Powered by a diesel-driven motor, sections of tubular-steel rods were driven into the ground, and the core was removed from the deepest one to show what was in the ground more than 100 feet below the surface. Fortunately the results confirmed the high hopes of a massive deposit with few if any faults, so the deal was ratified.

During this time I got to know the vice-president of US Gypsum, who was in charge of the operation. He said that their industry had one supremely favourable feature. Because the number of housing starts in the USA was published at frequent intervals, they could estimate correctly the demand for their products a few months ahead. I remembered this comment many years later when at

London and Manchester Assurance the occasions arose to invest in American common stocks. US Gypsum was always high on the list. Through the good offices of a stockbroker friend in Chicago, Winfield Ellis, I was able to call on the president, Graham Morgan, and learned at first hand how satisfied they were with the purchase of the Jamaican deposit.

It is a pleasant feature of American business life that the heads of big corporations are often very ready to meet stockholders and to discuss their affairs. Such meetings seldom if ever give rise to abuse through 'insider' dealings. I think this practice is on the increase in Great Britain and, in my opinion, should be encouraged.

The completion of the Jamaican sale took place after I had left Equity and Law, but I heard that the loan was repaid in full and a modest profit made from the Equity interests. Loudon did not live for many years afterwards, and Bellrock Gypsum Industries was later sold to the British Plaster Board Company. While the whole business may not have been very profitable for Equity and Law, it enabled a credit of some $2 million to accrue to the country's badly needed balance of payments – and I benefited from experience in an entirely new field.

After the war had ended I brooded over my future. The challenge of crisis was over, and my job was to make the society more and more prosperous, aiming at increasing the income and capital values of its invested assets. I was appointed to to the board in 1948, which widened my interests in the society, yet I felt there was something lacking, which I could not define satisfactorily to myself. So in 1953 I cut the painter and created a vacuum which sooner or later I would have to fill. Many kind new friends knew that I had 'sacked myself', and helped me into a variety of new occupations including a directorship of Associated Equipment Company (my first involvement with the motor industry), a seat on the board of Industrial and Commercial

Finance Corporation, a close involvement with the unit trust world through Save and Prosper, a membership of the Kuwait Investment Board, a directorship of Broadstone Investment Trust and, for a time, of the London Trust, and a return to the life assurance world through joining the board of the London and Manchester Assurance Co. Ltd.

London and Manchester Assurance Co. Ltd, 1953–78

I was appointed to the board of London and Manchester in June 1953. The catalyst was my good friend Donald Savory, who both as an actuary and as a stockbroker was widely recognized as the doyen of experts on insurance shares. Although there was no outward appearance of anything critically wrong with the company, Savory felt that it lacked the leavening of non-executive directors, for there were none at that time; he felt also that the company's affairs were too much under the influence of one particular family. So, primarily because of his intervention, Harold Rouse, who had just retired as chief general manager of the Midland Bank, and I were invited to join the board. As I was expected to take a close interest in investment matters I was first shown the list of the company's investments by the chairman, Sir Alfred Suenson-Taylor, who was about to be ennobled in the Coronation honours as Lord Grantchester.

The sight of this list perturbed me greatly. The British government securities were all irredeemable, and the amount of ordinary shares was very small. The nature of the life assurance business was predominantly short-term endowment, so assets and liabilities were basically mismatched. I hesitated for several days before accepting this new challenge, but once the decision was made I never had occasion to regret it.

At the outset I was asked to take the chair of a newly formed investment committee of the board. This close involvement was a considerable help to me in the task ahead. The top priority was to reduce the preponderance of irredeemables, but the terms on which this would be done were critically important. Panic sales at too low prices would jeopardize recovery, but in the event luck came to our rescue. Within a few months of June 1953 the bank rate was reduced from 4 per cent to 3 per cent, and 3½ per cent War Loan rose from the low 70s to about 90. In such circumstances judgement was hardly necessary: compulsion was strong enough, and very soon all government irredeemables were eliminated and reinvested either in redeemable stocks or in building up a substantial portfolio of ordinary shares. Here too fortune smiled, as the FT 30-share ordinary index was in the low 100s and the 'cult of the equity' was still in the future. In addition to a representative list of industrial, financial and other ordinary shares, investment trust shares looked particularly cheap, without undue risk, and in the circumstances appeared ideal for long-term investment; and that was the start of the heavy involvement which was later accumulated.

The London and Manchester Assurance was then one of the smaller industrial life offices, with funds just under £50 million split about half and half: industrial branch and ordinary branch. There was also a relatively small general branch where the risks were wholly reinsured with the County Fire Office. The industrial branch business, or home service insurance, as it was becoming named, was new territory to me, and I set to work to learn and understand its main features. I soon became aware of the high cost of weekly collection in the policy-holders' homes, and the poor financial return appalled me. It took a long time to appreciate the value of the home-service aspect, as distinct from the financial one. In the regular call at the policy-holder's home every week, many more subjects than insurance were discussed. The agent became a guide, counsellor and friend on various matters such as form-filling and so on, and not infrequently a personal confidant of the family.

There were two main ways open to improve the financial worth of the policy-holder's contract: economy and efficiency of administration; and improved return on the company's investments leading to a bigger participation in the surplus. The managing director at the time, Albert Mann, a hard-working and dedicated actuary, worked wonders in streamlining the work of the field staff. Collections were concentrated and overlapping avoided. More work was being done by fewer people, with economy for the company and a greater reward to the staff. The sharing of surplus between policy-holders and shareholders had been casual to such an extent that the articles of association were completely silent on the subject. In the ordinary branch, policy-holders were getting about 95 per cent of the distributable surplus, but in the industrial branch considerably less than 90 per cent. A steady progress to the more conventional 90:10 per cent share in each branch was made, and this ratio has been accepted practice ever since. In course of time the bonus to industrial branch policy-holders reached a point where some positive financial return was received, in addition to the costly but much valued home service also provided.

In the early days of the new regime begun in 1953 the chairman, Lord Grantchester, initiated three practices which proved to be of great value. He organized visits by the board to major cities to meet the officials in those areas. Informal personal dialogues took place and the non-executive directors, in particular, learned much of the problems of the field staff and their managers. Then every agent who increased his weekly collection by a certain minimum, £100 per week, was presented with a gold wristlet watch at a board meeting, when a friendly question-and-answer session took place.

The company was organized into about fifteen geographical divisions, each under a divisional manager. Every year a challenge cup was presented to the leading division in each branch and every member of the winning division joined in the celebrations at a luncheon, and latterly with their spouses at a dinner-dance. The intense competition which was generated did much to increase the total new business written by the company.

Within a few years the company had established a pattern of steady, undramatic progress and increasing prosperity; but soon some quite unexpected events occurred which had a profound effect on its future. At that time I had written a few articles which were published in the *Investor's Chronicle*, and in 1957 I was asked by the editor, Harold Wincott, to describe and comment on the practice which had been growing in America of linking the benefits of pensions to funds of equity shares. One of the leading American funds was the College Retirement Equities Fund, founded primarily for the staffs of universities. Some erudite investment researchers had proved that over many decades the movement of the retail price index had shown a close correlation with leading indices of equity shares. One should add, however, that this applies only during periods of mild changes in the retail price index. Once inflation approaches double figures government intervention, in the shape of controls of prices, profits, and dividends, tends to negate such correlation.

The Finance Act 1956, which gave tax relief to the self-employed who were providing for their own pensions, had just been passed, and it was timely to examine the possibilities of an equity-linked fund for the self-employed. For many reasons the most feasible method seemed to me to use an existing unit trust as the equity link. I thought investment trust units, run by Save and Prosper, would be the most appropriate one, because of its immensely wide spread of experienced investment management. I then asked my colleagues to draw up a blueprint of a contract where the contributions would be paid in sterling and the pension entitlement received in the currency of investment trust units. The scheme seemed practicable, but I had the greatest difficulty in persuading my colleagues to put it on the market. Novelty can be attractive to some but anathema to others. A major factor which tipped the balance in favour was the enthusiasm of Willis, Faber & Dumas Ltd, one of the largest insurance broking firms in London, who proved as good as their word in their backing of the scheme. This was the first equity-linked contract of its kind launched in Great Britain, and it caused much comment and interest in insurance circles.

The Life Offices Association did not like the departure from the conventional sterling contract, and its members after due deliberation resolved not to imitate such a contract without giving advance notice to all its members. Surely this was a unique example of a company's being handed a near-monopoly by its competitors. But sadly the company was lukewarm in its attempts to sell it. Little was done in the way of advertising or other publicity. Now, one cannot open a Sunday paper without seeing pages and pages of advertisements of equity-linked contracts.

However, when this contract came of age, twenty-one years later, it was possible to state that over that period the price of investment trust units had increased nearly six times – a greater rise than the rate of inflation over the same period. Furthermore, the fund had contributed in 1982 £700,000 to profit and loss account. The excess of caution at the inception illustrates that no worthwhile reward can be obtained without some degree of risk. As originator and chief protagonist of this contract I made a cardinal mistake in not insisting that the pros and cons were formally debated at the board table, with individual opinions being minuted, instead of being confined to off-the-record discussions.

Another development was the introduction of the Endowment Share Purchase Plan, under which money was lent to borrowers with an assured income on the security of an eligible list of investment trust equities and unit trusts, accompanied by a life policy as collateral. The scheme was devised jointly by an insurance broker, Harry Peace of Morice Tozer & Co., and the company. It was designed to help those with a good income but little capital to accumulate capital through regular saving, and hopefully to achieve some investment appreciation.

In 1958 Peter Thorneycroft, who had resigned as Chancellor of the Exchequer in what his Prime Minister, Harold Macmillan, described at the time as 'a little local difficulty', joined the board. He was a delightful and helpful colleague, and added considerably to the company's prestige. When he returned to the government in 1960 as Minister of Aviation, to lay the foundation among other things of Concorde, he was succeeded by Nigel Birch (later Lord Rhyl), who until his retirement in 1977 was at all times a tower of strength and a fount of wisdom.

The events of the last five paragraphs no doubt had much influence on the next event of moment to the company. In 1961, without any preliminary flirtation, the Eagle Star Insurance approached Lord Grantchester with proposals to take over the London and Manchester. When the proposals were submitted to the board they did not commend themselves either from a structural business point of view or by their financial terms. Although they were rejected officially by the whole board, Lord Grantchester viewed the matter in a very different light from his colleagues. After much discussion he resigned as chairman, and I was invited to succeed him. I had never held any ambitions in this direction, indeed the thought had never occurred to me, but in all the circumstances it seemed cowardly to refuse. I had no illusions about the immediate difficulties, since it was not yet public knowledge that the Eagle Star had made an approach. (The take-over panel and its rules had not yet been formed.) Lord Grantchester took the initiative with the press, while I remained silent but got most of the backlash. It was a difficult and unpleasant time for me, yet I was wonderfully sustained by the support of my other colleagues, especially Nigel Birch, and, once they were told the full facts, also by the management.

I remember being telephoned at home by a City editor at about one o'clock one morning, enquiring if I had seen what was in one of the next day's papers. I replied somewhat acidly that I didn't usually get the morning papers until 7.30 a.m. The item of news was the formation of a shareholders' committee under the chairmanship of Lord Tenby to urge the company to reopen discussions with the Eagle Star. I welcomed the formation of this committee as it would provide a forum to explain the company's views, and I sought an early meeting. Several meetings took place and ended with a joint letter being sent to all the shareholders, over the signatures of myself and Lord Tenby, conveying the considered opinion that no useful purpose would be served by reopening the matter.

The affair received wide publicity in the press – there could not have been much competing news at the time – and probably did the company more good than harm. It certainly put everyone in the company on their mettle to prove that it could continue to flourish as an independent organization. An obvious move for any new chairman in such circumstances would be to enlarge and strengthen the board, and in late 1961 Keith Browne, the secretary of the company at the time, and Denys Oppé of Kleinwort Benson joined the board. It was further strengthened five years later by Christopher Loder (now Lord Wakehurst), who was then with Charter Consolidated.

One of my earlier tasks as chairman was a thorough examination of the chief office in Finsbury Square. This had been built in three stages: the first in the last century; the next in the early part of this century; and the last in the 1940s. The interconnections were not good, even the floor

45

levels being inconsistent, and the sub-basements where the old files and deeds were kept in an appalling condition. Deed-boxes were rusting, cobwebs abounded, and I suspect vermin were never far away. It was so bad that something radical would undoubtedly have to be done.

The only question was whether to modernize the two oldest parts or to make a clean sweep, demolishing everything and starting afresh. After much deliberation and consultation with professional advisers we decided on the latter course. But a complete rebuilding would involve the leasing of temporary premises for about three years, which even under the most favourable circumstances would not be an easy task. Yet we were lucky. We found suitable offices in neighbouring Finsbury Circus and were able to trade our requirement of a short lease for the landlord's needs of long-term finance. In the event the long-term proved to be short-term, since, soon after we moved out, the property was sold and our loan repaid. The rate of interest on this loan was well below the rate ruling at the time of repayment.

We were fortunate in securing the services of Fitzroy Robinson as architect of the new building. His instructions were to design a functional building with character, to the best modern standards, and to the maximum capacity allowed by the planning authorities. We were in advance of the times in providing for air-conditioning: sited as we were, on a noisy corner, it had been impossible to hear over the telephone with windows open.

The contract, worth about £1,250,000, was put out to competitive tender and was awarded to G. E. Wallis & Co. In addition to their reputation for work of good quality, they were the right size of firm – big enough to handle a task of this size, yet not too big for it to be other than very important to them. The building was completed and occupied in 1966, and an excellent job was done by all parties concerned. Nearly ten years later we found this new building to be the best large investment ever made by the company: it was sold to Canadian Pacific for £11 million.

The new chief office undoubtedly increased the efficiency of the organization and did much also to enhance the prestige of the company. We settled down to another stage of steady, good, though undramatic progress. Like many other life offices we gave from time to time special reversionary bonuses arising out of investment appreciation. This practice was taken a step further in 1967 when the actuary, Alan Wilson, devised a system whereby, instead of intermittent write-ups of assets every few years, each participating policy-holder benefited when the policy became a claim in more direct relation to the individual contributions. The amount of terminal bonus was calculated automatically, according to the investment experience, and was not dependent on the discretion of the board.

In 1967, following the retirement of Albert Mann, Keith Browne was appointed managing director. Subsequently a special board meeting was held one evening with the sole item on the agenda being the longer-term planning of the company. (This is a practice which could be followed usefully by most organizations.) We came to the conclusion that, while we did not aspire to become one of the giants, we were smaller than an optimum level of economic efficiency. We accordingly decided to keep our eyes open to acquire any smaller company which might fit in well with our own. After one or two frustrated attempts we learned that the owners of Welfare Insurance were anxious to sell, and this possibility called for immediate investigation.

Welfare's headquarters were in Folkestone. The sole owners were Edward Bates (Holdings), who had bought Welfare a few years earlier from its founders, Brooke Bond Liebig. So one autumn day in 1974 Keith Browne, David Jubb (deputizing for the actuary, George Tyrrell, who was on sick leave), and I went by train to Folkestone with representatives of Bates travelling in an adjoining compartment. We were met by John Owen, chairman of Welfare, Alan Philips, managing director, and Dennis Baker, his deputy. We split up, with Browne examining the general organization and type of business, Jubb making the best estimate of the amount of the liabilities, greatly helped by Welfare's assistant actuary, Tom Pyne, while I concentrated on the assets. When the three of us met to compare notes at lunch we all hoped that a viable proposition would emerge, but at the end of the day our findings pointed to an estimated deficiency of about £2 million. We informed the Bates people, who had been waiting anxiously in an adjoining room, and who were naturally disappointed, though not altogether surprised. We returned sadly to London, feeling that Welfare was not for us and that we would hear nothing more about its affairs. But the next day Keown-Boyd, the chief executive of Bates, asked to see me and enquired whether, if Bates were to put £2 million additional capital into Welfare, we would be prepared to buy the company for a token consideration of, say, £50,000. This would be the price for acquiring a company with an annual premium income of about £10 million. The risks were obvious but the possibilities of gain were enormous, should we succeed in putting the business to rights.

The London and Manchester board boldly accepted the recommendation of their investigating colleagues and heads of agreement were signed. The relief was felt in a much wider circle than amongst those most immediately concerned, reaching the staff, the policy-holders, and the Department of Trade. At that time financial confidence was at a very low ebb, the stock market was acutely nervous, and two small life assurance companies had already failed. The failure of Welfare would have had grave repercussions over a wide area.

When the heads of agreement had been agreed in draft, Bates pressed strongly to make them binding. While the London and Manchester proceeded in complete good faith, the preamble cited the understanding that the deficiency was about £2 million, and the interval between signing the heads of agreement and completion of the full agreement would allow the necessary time to make a more reliable estimate. So London and Manchester insisted that the heads should not be binding, and Bates reluctantly assented. It was deemed fitting that Browne, Jubb and I should immediately join the board of Welfare, and that I should take the chair. One of my first tasks was to meet all the senior staff of Welfare at Folkestone, to explain what was happening, and to tell them some of our hopes for the future. We then got to work to assess more accurately the amount of the assets and the liabilities. This was a difficult task, as a large proportion of the assets were in speculative properties and in mortgages where the property in mortgage was also speculative. When we got a more reliable estimate the deficiency was found to be substantially greater than the £2 million first estimated.

Obviously this changed the whole picture, and we kept the Department of Trade fully informed. The Department, which was advised by the government actuary's department, did its utmost to save the day, hoping among other things that Bates could be persuaded to put up more money. I thought it right to write to Keown-Boyd setting out the minimum terms on which a deal might still be possible. This would involve a larger cash injection of new capital, or part cash and part loan on very favourable terms. Before Bates replied, the Department of Trade summoned a meeting of all interested parties, including Welfare's bankers, the National Westminster Bank, and the chairman of the Life Offices Association (though Welfare was not a member). I shall never forget that meeting. It began at 11 a.m. and broke up at about 2.30 p.m.; no refreshments of any kind were provided, but it sowed the seeds of a happy outcome. Soon afterwards Bates replied saying no, and almost immediately after that the board of Welfare

passed a resolution for voluntary liquidation. They had no
alternative. Then events moved with lightning speed.

Sidney Wild, deputy chief executive of the National
Westminster Bank, had been at the long meeting at the
Department of Trade. His bank had made a substantial total
of loans to parents for payment of school fees, repayable
ultimately out of endowment assurance policies issued by
Welfare. Two thoughts had been forming in his mind: first,
the effect on the security of those loans if Welfare failed; and
second, if loans on favourable terms by Bates could have
saved the day, why shouldn't his bank make such loans
rather than see Welfare fail, with all the consequences that
this would involve? Within a few hours of the Welfare
board's resolution to wind up, Wild asked to see me
urgently, and spelt out his thoughts, stressing that if they
were to be implemented his bank would want some share in
Welfare's capital. I immediately telephoned Welfare's
chairman, John Owen, and asked him to defer their decision, which was done, while a new agreement was thrashed
out. At this stage Brooke Bond Liebig came into the picture. The pensions of many of its staff were still dependent
upon the viability of Welfare, and thus the company had a
vested interest in its survival. It was thought fair therefore
that Brooke Bond Liebig should join in the provision of
loan money on favourable terms.

With exemplary speed, heads of agreement were drawn
up under which Bates subscribed £2 million of fresh capital
to Welfare and sold the whole of the capital of Welfare for
£50,000: 51 per cent to London and Manchester and 49 per
cent to National Westminster Bank. That bank provided £2
million and Brooke Bond Liebig £500,000 of loan money
on very favourable terms to Welfare, repayable within five
years out of future surplus. Some £250,000 of pensions in
payment were also deferred for twelve months as an additional contribution from Brooke Bond Liebig, who in turn
made good this deferment. National Westminster Bank

would have two representatives on the board of Welfare, though it was agreed that London and Manchester would supervise its management. When this agreement came up for ratification by the two boards there could have been no great enthusiasm, though both were no doubt fully aware of the grave damage to general confidence which failure to implement would have involved. So both boards confirmed, and one significant life assurance company which had been 'on the brink' was saved. The story of its restoration to health and the part it played in the London and Manchester Group will be told in the next sections.

Welfare Insurance Co. Ltd, 1974-78

At the end of 1974 we set to work. The new board comprised: three former Welfare directors, Owen, Philips and Baker, though the first two resigned at an early date; Tom McMillan and Peter Jacobs from National Westminster Bank, to be followed later by Philip Wilkinson, all of whom were to prove to be delightful, dedicated and valuable colleagues; from London and Manchester, Browne and Jubb, with myself as chairman. We agreed at the outset to tackle our task in three stages: (1) First aid; (2) Convalescence; (3) Vigorous and healthy expansion.

The obvious first step was to stop doing all the things that had been responsible for the company's deficiency. There were many similarities with what I had met at Equity and Law. There was a vast inflow of new money in the form of single premiums, though in Welfare they were called 'bonds', either growth or income, with guaranteed surrender values. This money had been placed for the greater part in term mortgages, and in the search for high yields the security was seldom first class; neither could they be realized at any realistic price. Indeed, shortly before London and Manchester came on the scene a large block of doubtful mortgages had been foreclosed by mutual agreement of lender and borrower.

All unprofitable business was stopped, where possible, and the remuneration of many insurance brokers was renegotiated. (Welfare was not a member of the Life Offices Association.) Owing to the shock to confidence, a much reduced level of new business would have to await the return to financial health. The critical problem lay firstly in augmenting both the capital and the income of the invested assets and secondly in trying to collect substantial amounts of initial commissions paid to brokers under 'indemnity' terms but not earned. The influx of the new £4,500,000 was most timely. We had taken the view that the equity market was on the turn, and where possible we hurried into that market.

A very substantial part of the company's business was in equity-linked contracts; the most important was the investment trust fund, which had been nearly fully invested at the beginning of 1974, and was nominally over 90 per cent liquid at the end of the year. As the market had fallen throughout 1974, this produced one of the best 'performances' in the equity-linked world, though one wonders whether such a good decision would have been made if the company had not been in trouble. In practice, all available liquidity and many saleable assets had been used to finance the payment, present and expected, of guaranteed surrender values under the 'bonds' referred to earlier. But it meant, now that we were taking an optimistic view of the market, that this excessive liquidity had to be invested quickly. In spite of the narrowness of markets for investment trust stocks, good progress was made, but it used up a substantial part of the new cash.

While the performance of the investment trust fund was favourable, that of the property fund was not. A very large investment had been made in a speculative property in Mayfair. Provided planning permission could be obtained for a substantial increase in letting space, and providing tenants could be obtained for all the space at full rents, then the proverbial 'gold mine' might be found. But none of these favourable events occurred and the board was left to nurse this unpromising baby. The only hope of recovering the lost money would be to find an equally speculative proposition which might prove a winner instead of a loser, but 'once bitten, twice shy'. However, at that time, after the collapse of the property market, the shares of most property companies were quoted at prices representing unduly low percentages of their asset values. Since shares were also eligible for inclusion in the property fund portfolio, we thought they would be the best vehicle for recovering some of the losses, and we gave effect to this policy, including the realization of the Mayfair property at its disappointing market value.

In those early days I received many letters of complaint from disappointed property-fund holders. It would have been stupid as well as wrong to hold out any false hopes, so the only sensible course was to admit to past 'errors of judgement' and to outline the policy for the future. Admission of past mistakes can often do much to assuage criticism.

The worst headache of all concerned a property not in the property fund. Welfare had previously financed a property development company, one of whose ventures was the acquisition of a large number of Victorian terraced houses in west London, with grandiose schemes of redevelopment as shops and offices. As a consequence of the agreed fore-closure, Welfare owned these undesirable residences, which brought in hardly any income at all. After a frustrated attempt to sell to the local authority we examined the possibility of a major and costly rehabilitation scheme, but professional advice was against it. Within a year or so we sold to a housing association at what seemed a fair value but was about one quarter of the original cost, which was about £4,250,000. The proceeds were put to much better and more productive use in the equity share market.

Nearly all investment markets improved in 1975, and by the end of that year the board was reasonably satisfied with the progress. The auditors, however, could not share that satisfaction to the full. The short-term loans of £2,500,000 were due for repayment within four years out of future surplus, and the auditors quite naturally could not certify that a sufficient amount of surplus would be earned, though the directors could express their opinion that there was no reason why it should not be earned. And so the auditors' report was 'qualified'. Although we were approaching Stage 2, Convalescence, a new cloud appeared on the horizon. New statutory regulations for valuing assets of insurance companies were about to be implemented. The first disallowed the practice, employed by Welfare and many other insurance offices, of valuing all term mortgages at face value. They had in future to be valued at the current rate of interest; thus, for example, a 9 per cent mortgage repayable in eight years' time with the current market rate being 12 per cent had to be valued at the appropriate discount. Owing to the large amount of term mortgages this new rule would hurt Welfare badly. The authorities were empowered to defer the implementation of this regulation if good cause could be shown. Welfare applied for deferment, confidently expecting that it would be granted.

This 'cloud' appeared much more menacing in the eyes of London and Manchester Assurance, for there was a nasty provision in the relevant act that where an insurance company was not wholly solvent according to the current regulations, and if controlled by another insurance company, the controlling company could not pay any dividend at all. This meant that if Welfare were not wholly solvent under this new regulation at the time of London and Manchester's annual general meeting, no dividend could legally be declared. So deferment of the new regulations became critically important. A lengthy dialogue with the Department of Trade took place, but the Department was understandably wary about establishing a precedent. Stock markets were highly sensitive at this time, partly because the Prime Minister, Harold Wilson, had just announced his intention to retire, and a few weeks would elapse before his successor – and his political inclinations – could be known.

As time passed and no favourable response from the Department of Trade seemed imminent, I thought it wise to prepare for the 'worst case' outcome. So I wrote a long letter to the Department outlining the various options open to London and Manchester and Welfare, and commenting on each of them in turn. If everything went wrong, and if we were faced with the likelihood of having to defer the London and Manchester's dividend, I would seek to sell 2 per cent of the London and Manchester's holding of Welfare, leaving 49 per cent, to our largest (and friendly) shareholder, thus making Welfare no longer technically a subsidiary. I do not know whether this letter influenced the Department's decision, but it was a relief to my immediate colleagues and myself, and enabled us to manage Welfare in a positive, hopeful manner and not to be continually on the defensive. The official letter granting the requested deferment arrived about noon on the day of the London and Manchester's annual general meeting due half an hour later, although we had been told a few days earlier that it was coming. In fact we had worried unnecessarily since we believed that Welfare was wholly solvent during all this critical time, even allowing for the imposition of the new regulations, though we could never be sure of the position a few days ahead.

Obviously we kept this predicament highly secret, and fortunately no investment analyst or financial writer spotted it, though knowledge of the published regulations and intelligent deduction might have detected it. But we were not completely in the clear, for the second lot of regulations were imminent. These, the admissibility rules, limited the percentage of total non-linked assets which would be taken credit for in any one individual investment. For example, in Welfare's case, if the limit for any one mortgage was £1 million, and £3 million happened to be invested in a single mortgage, then that mortgage, however sound the security, could not be valued in excess of £1 million. If these regulations had been brought in, say, five years earlier, Welfare would probably not have got into the trouble it did. We ruefully contemplated that this was a case of locking the stable door after the horse had bolted.

We were warned by the Department of Trade that no similar deferment could be granted in respect of the new admissibility rule. Solving the problem by seeking to dispose of any excess to a third party was for practical reasons out of the question. The only solution was to transfer at fair value any such excess to the larger parent company; but this would only be a practical policy if London and Manchester were to own 100 per cent of Welfare.

So discussions started with the National Westminster Bank, which readily accepted the realities of the situation. An agreement was reached under which London and Manchester would buy the bank's 49 per cent holding of Welfare at its cost price, to be satisfied in London and Manchester shares at current market value. In addition, as a 'sweetener', London and Manchester offered the bank an option on 75,000 London and Manchester shares at 145p per share – a modest premium over the ruling quotation at the time. The agreement was ratified by both boards and by the shareholders of London and Manchester in an extraordinary general meeting.

The way was then open for a massive rearrangement of assets and liabilities between London and Manchester and its wholly owned subsidiary, Welfare, and which eliminated any excess of inadmissible assets.

Another important extension of this agreement gave the

ability to expand rapidly in the area of pensions, where Welfare had the expertise; but doubts still remained, especially among the larger City insurance brokers, about its financial strength. Policies could now be issued by London and Manchester reassured with Welfare. By the end of 1977 further recovery had taken place in the value of Welfare's assets (and also the income therefrom) and an early repayment of 20 per cent (£500,000), of the short-term loans could be made. (All the £2,500,000 loans have since been repaid.) After many trials and anxieties Welfare had become a valuable and promising part of the London and Manchester group, a subsidiary which had been bought when it was on its knees for £50,000, with an annual premium income of £10 million, and with the proven ability to earn a surplus, in one year at any rate, of over £500,000. Its value now to London and Manchester has been independently assessed at £6·125 million.

London and Manchester Assurance Group, 1974–78

The London and Manchester Assurance and Welfare Insurance began to operate as a group soon after the latter became a wholly owned subsidiary.

This grouping became manifest in two important ways. First, some of the managers became group appointments – group actuary, group accountant, and so on. Secondly, plans were made to locate the chief office administration in one place instead of two. About five years previously the London and Manchester board had agreed in principle to move out of London and set up a chief office far away from the London commuter belt. This decision had to be kept secret from the staff until the new location was decided, as there would have been no point in disturbing them until it was known where the new venue would be. So a small team scoured the country by rail, road and latterly by aeroplane, to seek the ideal place. After many frustrating months they found and recommended the purchase and development of Winslade Park, an old mansion in extensive grounds at Clyst St Mary, a few miles from Exeter. Sir Philip Powell of Powell and Moya was appointed architect to adapt the mansion and to construct a modern office complex in the attractive grounds.

Before the staff were told, an attractive illustrated brochure was prepared, describing the new site and giving full information about housing, schools, hospitals, recreation, and so on, as well as the financial considerations, such as payment of removal expenses, mortgage facilities and provision for early retirement for those approaching retirement age. The chief reasons for the move were the worsening travel conditions in the London commuter area, a healthier environment in the country, and ultimately a considerable saving in costs of administration.

Within the previous five years Welfare had moved out of London to Folkestone and the staff had settled happily in that area. Most of them were reluctant to move again, even if to another delightful area, but they saw the logic of concentrating in one headquarters. In May 1978 Winslade Park was formally opened and the chief office staffs of the group moved in. A small office was retained in London for board meetings and for some senior executives.

During this period of expansion the board had been augmented and strengthened by John Thomson, an executive director of Brooke Bond Liebig, John Peyton MP, a former minister of transport in Edward Heath's government, and Sir Ronald McIntosh, who had recently retired as director-general of the National Economic Development Office.

In 1978 an important decision was made in the general branch. All risks had been wholly reinsured with the Sun Alliance and London Insurance Ltd. It was announced that the treaty of reinsurance would be renegotiated with a view to the London and Manchester Group's taking a more active participation in the underwriting risks. In preparation for this, fresh capital of about £2 million was raised by means of a rights issue.

To sum up, the group funds had by 1982 reached a total of over £600 million. It was actively engaged in virtually all aspects of insurance. It gave promise in its new location of operating at an economic level of expenditure. The group was almost unrecognizable from the London and Manchester of a quarter of a century ago.

At the time of the move, consideration was given to a possible change in the name of the company, as many might expect – I don't think I am revealing any 'classified' information. Manchester had never played a significant part in the company, and the title had no charismatic appeal. Many alternatives were thought of, but in the end it was decided to retain the present name. London and Manchester Assurance had built up goodwill and prestige under that name, especially in recent years, and it seemed wrong to jeopardize that benefit. While I might have wished the company to have been born with a different name, I am sure the decision to retain its century-old title was the correct one.

When I retired from active involvement with life assurance in May 1978 I had the satisfaction of having worked for three companies: Equity and Law; London and Manchester; and Welfare, all of which in different ways had at times been in serious trouble, but without any doubt Welfare was for me the most satisfying. Much skill was required from all who held responsible positions, and we were also blessed with a great deal of good luck, which is an essential part of any rescue operation, and I like to think that my earlier experience with companies in trouble was of value. Nothing could have been achieved without the help, skill and companionship of my colleagues at all levels, and to each and all I remain deeply grateful.

CHAPTER 3

Investment

Investment is both an art and a science. The art springs from practice, the science from theory. They can seldom be separated. Indeed, it is difficult to isolate any aspect of investment and discuss it separately. I propose therefore to relate my experiences of investment, and the lessons I have learned, in chronological order.

1928–30

My introduction to investment occurred when I was working in the Scottish Amicable Life Assurance Society in Glasgow. I was the only clerk in the investment department, so I always knew what was done, but only occasionally knew why it was done.

That time was the heyday of the formation of investment trust companies in the west of Scotland. The usual practice was for the capital to be issued in the form of £10 shares, payable by instalments. When fully paid, the shares were split, usually into £6 5 per cent cumulative preference stock and £4 ordinary stock. Soon afterwards, debenture stock would be issued for an amount equal to the full share capital, typically a 5 per cent stock issued at a small discount. The ordinary stock was thus highly geared. Since in those days it was possible to earn at least 6 per cent with reasonable safety, on a mixed portfolio of investments, a rate of earnings on the ordinary of about 10 per cent was not difficult to attain. This was one of the factors responsible for the normal quotation of ordinary stock being at a premium over its asset value. The other main factor was that the demand for such investment trust ordinaries was greater than the supply. The demand came from both the private investor and the insurance companies, each of which greatly valued the benefit of experienced management and the spread of investment over a wide area. The directors were all experienced in investment affairs, though no better than the present generation, when the supply of investment trust stocks is so much greater than the demand; hence the large discounts currently ruling between market values and asset values.

In the late 1920s investment of life assurance funds, compared to present times, was uncomplicated. Equity investment was in its infancy, and in the Scottish Amicable was confined almost entirely to investment trusts. There was a keen desire to invest in the USA, but until the Wall Street crash in 1929 investment was confined to preferred stocks and shares, largely because common stocks were considered too risky and too highly priced.

On the morrow of the Wall Street crash in the autumn of 1929 the investment supremo, the general manager, William Hutton, decided that the opportunity had come to buy American common stocks at attractive levels. He selected about ten stocks and placed buying limits well below the ruling prices. To his colleagues' amazement, though probably not to his own, most of the stocks were then bought at these keen limits. In a demoralized market, where large quantities were held on borrowed money, any firm bid that was somewhere near the market price was welcome to frightened holders who often had their bank managers breathing down their necks. In all it was a brilliant operation for a life assurance society making its first entry into the

American equity market. Soon afterwards a rally took place and several of these purchases showed substantial gains.

The general manager then recommended to his board that where the best gains were obtained those stocks should be sold. I was told that one non-executive director countered with the question that, if it was right to sell on a technical rally, why should we not sell all the recent purchases, whether the profit was large or small, or even at an exceptional loss? This view was accepted and all were sold, giving a substantial overall profit: and the tactics proved sound, since the sustained recovery did not start until about three years later.

This was my first lesson in the doctrine that the future of any investment is independent of the price anyone paid for it in the past. It is sometimes difficult to remember this tenet, though it is little different from the fallacy that if you toss a coin ten times and it turns up heads each time then the eleventh throw is more likely to be tails because of the so-called 'law of averages'. Once one starts to think about it, the answer is that the odds on each throw is always evens, and that the 'law of averages' is only fully valid in infinity. Good memory is usually a virtue, but in investment matters ignorance of past actions can at times be a benefit.

To conclude this section in lighter vein, a word on the practice of placing orders with stockbrokers. Long-distance telephone calls were hardly ever used. Instructions to London brokers were occasionally given by letter, usually by telegram, and the telegram was normally channelled through the society's London office. It was customary to fix a dealing limit, and after the figure the phrase 'or better' was always added. Indeed, on the few occasions I had to draft the telegram myself, I was under standing orders to add the phrase. I imagine the reason was to encourage the broker to try extra hard, though I doubt it ever had any effect on the outcome. I would like to relate that the instructions were given: 'at best, or better'. But that never happened, for some limit had always to be given. Fortunately, today, communications between institutional client and broker are closer and founded on much greater mutual understanding.

1930–40

I moved to London in July 1930 and joined Buckmaster & Moore, stockbrokers. They were in the vanguard of a new practice then in stockbroking circles which gave priority to offering good advice, which was deemed more important than dealing marginally better than a competitor. This involved research and statistical analysis.

One of the most outstanding examples of good advice which I recollect having witnessed was with the Argentine Railways. Thomas Balogh (now Lord Balogh) had joined the firm in the research field. Helped no doubt by his Central European familiarity with depreciating currencies, he formed the view that the Argentine peso was overvalued and would soon depreciate. He followed this view through to observing the disastrous effect that such devaluation would have on the earnings of the railways, which had been financed almost entirely by sterling capital and sterling debt, and strongly recommended a sale. As nearly every investment institution had holdings of Argentine Railway stocks, and some of them very substantial ones, the scope for business was large. Most acted on the advice given, and the whole operation was brilliantly successful. It was a perfect example of good investment research, which is basically to foresee some major event and translate its happening into the effect on the related investment securities, an important corollary being to examine also what would happen if the expected event did not take place. In short, the penalty of being wrong was relevant as well as the reward of being right.

One of my own assignments was the study of railway securities, especially home and Indian. In those days home

63

rails comprised several issues – debenture, preference and ordinary – of the four main-line companies: Great Western, LMS, LNER and Southern. The annual reports often ran to about a hundred pages, containing detailed statistics of operations, and during the year weekly traffic returns kept me up to date. There was thus considerable scope for the analyst.

Most of the Indian railways had been nationalized in the era of the First World War. Compensation had been made in the form of terminable annuities ending in the late 1940s. The 'A' annuities were of £1 per annum, and the market value reflected the value of a fixed annuity at the ruling rate of interest. They had a very limited appeal. The 'B' annuities gave an annual income of a few shillings, and the remainder of the £1 was invested by trustees in a sinking fund to provide a captial sum on termination. The investments of the sinking fund were published and the policy of the trustees was usually known. The largest, Great Indian Peninsular Railway 'B' annuities, was subject to the policy of the trustees investing chiefly in their own GIP 'B' annuities. Calculation of the expected repayment on termination was, therefore, an involved and complicated matter, unlikely to have been expounded in any financial journal.

The two most important Indian railways then left in the private sector carried the glamorous names of Bengal and North Western Railway and Rohilkund and Kumaon Railway. The reports were informative and traffic returns were published monthly. The ordinary stocks of the two companies proved to be high yielding and relatively safe investments – but that was in the 'days of the Raj', and before competition from road and air had become serious.

At times I got involved in the study of American railroads, and, on the subject of glamorous names, what could be more so than Atchison Topeka and Santa Fe Railway? Certainly when contrasted with that present hybrid of public and private enterprise – Conrail!

I got a good general education in investment matters during this decade in the City. Markets were desperately depressed during the ensuing three years or so. It is more pleasant to be initiated in a boom, but not nearly so instructive. I benefited greatly from close contact with the firm's most prestigious client, John Maynard Keynes. He was not only the leading economist of his time, but was also a very shrewd investor. He did not rely solely on his economic expertise, but recognized that the price of a security is mainly influenced by what 'the average person today thinks the average person will think in a few months' time'. Such reasoning does not always lend itself to erudite study.

On his return from a visit to America in, I think, 1933, when the stock market was desperately demoralized, he gave a talk to some members of the firm. He had been bargain-hunting with supreme confidence, saying that it was 'just a question of waiting until people returned to their senses'. He told us with great pleasure that he had bought a bond at the price of its coupon: default was expected, but did not happen. This must have been a unique example of a 100 per cent yield right from the start.

In 1931 Great Britain abandoned the gold standard and devalued. The National Government was formed, the Ottawa agreements brought in a limited amount of protection, and a cheap money policy enabled 5 per cent War Loan to be converted to a 3½ per cent loan. For the next five years or so an aura of prosperity returned to the country, with a rising stock market. However, immediately after the devaluation and against the background of a world recession, the firm decided that the best investment for speculative private investors was not in the stock market but in the commodity markets, especially wheat. It then proceeded to buy wheat futures for its clients on a vast scale, which in time proved to be a very wide decision. One statistically minded member of the firm calculated that its clients had accumulated enough wheat to feed the whole country for six weeks. Unfortunately, in the euphoria following a correct judgement, carelessness crept in. I remember the shock when one morning a cable arrived saying that the firm's cargo of wheat was due to be discharged at Tilbury the next day and asking for instructions about taking delivery. A frantic effort was needed to sell this cargo for 'spot' and repurchase for 'forward' delivery.

In the latter part of the 1930s the most powerful market factor was the growing threat of war and the occasional temporary relief – witness the state of the markets a few days before and a few days after the Munich Agreement.

With the benefit of hindsight, I now see that I stayed in the City longer than I needed. One of the most valuable lessons I learned there was to understand the difficulties of dealing. Many an investment manager has been dismayed when he wanted to buy or sell, say, 10,000 shares and found that after dealing in 1000 or 2000 shares the price moved sharply against him. Several stockbroking firms welcome and give facilities for institutional investors to spend a few months in their firm to learn and understand the techniques of dealing, and I believe that in the interests of all concerned such a move is greatly to be desired. I, for one, felt the benefit.

1940–53

I took up my duties as investment manager of Equity and Law Life Assurance Society in April 1940. The report and accounts for the year to 31 December 1939 raised no overt fears for the company's solvency, yet indicated that safety margins were slender. This meant that no undue risks could be run with the investment portfolio; indeed, 'safety first' was the compelling motto. However, even against the background of such restraints it was surprising how many opportunities were presented to improve the situation. It was obvious that low interest rates would prevail during wartime, with the government having the ability to enforce them. Thus medium-dated or long-dated stocks were to be preferred to short-dated ones. All short-dated stocks in the portfolio, where they were quoted near the maturity figure, were successfully sold, even during the worst of times. I remember being amazed when a limit to sell Melbourne & Metropolitan Tramways 5 per cent stock (due for redemption within a few years) at 98 was actually realized within a few hours of the French surrender.

In the process of eliminating some of the less promising investments I came up against a practical difficulty. The board almost without exception thought it was fundamentally wrong to sell any investment at a loss, and as most were showing a loss such restraint would point to doing virtually nothing. I therefore adopted the device of showing, when reporting a sale, the market price at 31 December 1939 as well as the cost price and pointing out that if the sale price was an improvement over the last recorded valuation we were moving in the right direction. Soon less attention was paid to cost price, which, as I have already indicated in another section, should have no bearing on the future.

As the fortunes of war began to improve after 1940, so did the financial markets, and gradually the society could adopt a less defensive and more positive policy. There was no consistent long-term policy – it was more a matter of responding to opportunities as they occurred – until near the end of the war, when a major campaign to buy investment trusts was started, which continued for many years. I was encouraged here in a curious way. The society had a subsidiary, not wholly owned, called Reserves Securities Trust Ltd, a small investment trust, on the board of which I was put in a non-executive capacity. The managing director, Edward Baring-Gould, had a penchant for investment trusts; indeed, he bought hardly anything else. I thought at the time that this policy was entirely wrong for an investment trust, and I used such phrases as 'cannibalism' and 'pig on pork'. In course of time I began to observe how profitable and worry-free these investments were turning out to be. The discounts between market price and asset value were large and became even larger when dividend limitation became more permanent in Mr Attlee's post-war government. I soon adopted all the enthusiasm of an ardent convert and started buying for the society, but the supply was small and accumulation was slow. This was probably the first occasion when I realized that the best investments are often those that are most difficult to buy. The converse is even truer.

The discounts were at times enormous, even by today's standards. I remember buying one stock at marginally over 100 when the asset value was about 250. This surely fell into Keynes's category of just waiting 'until people came to their senses'.

This persistent buying of investment trust stocks did not pass unnoticed by the boards of some of the companies whose stocks were being bought. One group, fearing a complete take-over (which we never envisaged), proposed that no one shareholding should exceed 10 per cent. The chairman and general manager of the Equity and Law thought it right to be neutral and to abstain from voting on the enabling resolution. When the matter came before the society's board, both chairman and general manager happened to be absent and the chair was taken by the deputy chairman, Lord Kennet, with myself as the senior official present. Before the meeting he asked me a direct question: 'Is this right or wrong?' I replied that I believed it was wrong. 'In that case,' he rejoined, 'we should vote against it,' and he persuaded his board to do so. In the knowledge of this opposition the company did not proceed with its proposals.

I had a happy and good relationship with the board, and an effective way of investment management was evolved. All policy matters were fully debated and decisions taken at board meetings. Within the agreed policy the investment manager was given a free hand, with all transactions being reported, and where appropriate explained, at the fortnightly meetings. I remember only one occasion when I felt keenly frustrated. Shortly after the end of the war I had a hunch that the Japanese would honour in full all their sterling debt. As the stocks were then quoted in the 30–40 per cent range, and with substantial arrears, I thought them a promising bargain and started to make modest purchases. When they were reported, with the recommendation to continue, I was strongly opposed and had to stop. I did not make the best of the argument, which was that the will could be more important than the ability, and that in this case 'saving face' was paramount. There are a few countries which, perhaps against expectation, have in time always honoured their foreign debt – Finland, Japan, Portugal, Thailand, Spain. I was told that many years ago Stanley Baldwin was being chided by his colleagues for having such a high proportion of the funds of the Bonar Law College at Ashridge invested in Finnish government stocks. He is alleged to have replied: 'Gallant little country, they will always pay up.' They did. In all investment matters the will to pay is often as important as the ability to pay.

1953–78

In June 1953 I joined the board of London and Manchester Assurance Company Ltd, and was appointed chairman of the investment committee, and later, in 1961, chairman of the company. Throughout this time I was in varying degrees involved with investment matters. The general strategy was comparatively uncomplicated. In 1953 too much was in irredeemable gilt-edged and too little in equities. When bank rate was cut from 4 to 3 per cent after I joined, the opportunity was presented to clear out of all irredeemables and reinvest either in dated stocks or in equities – the FT 30-share index being then in the low 100s. The arguments in favour of these moves were so compelling that debate was scarcely necessary. While leading industrials played a part in the equity portfolios, pride of place was given to investment trusts.

As soon as a balanced portfolio had been achieved, the objective was to avoid and dispose of the losers and hunt for the winners. This sounds like an idle platitude, but opportunities arose from time to time to put it into practice, and I will give a few examples. Like most insurance companies we had a number of near-gilt-edged securities, local authority stocks, public boards, and the like. One day, I think in the 1960s, we listed them and compared the yields with comparable British government stocks. We found the improvement in yield was tiny, about ⅛ per cent, and we formed the opinion that such improvement was not nearly adequate compensation for the poorer marketability and the slight extra risk involved. So we decided as a matter of policy to sell the lot.

A few years later, in the early 1970s, Mersey Docks and Harbour Board got into trouble and defaulted. We realized then that we had acted better than we had thought at the time. I asked the investment department to confirm that all Mersey Docks holdings had been sold, and received a qualified affirmative. One stock, a very short-dated one, had not been sold because it had not been quoted in the official list. When on the morrow of default we tried to negotiate a sale at any reasonable price we found to our great surprise that the stock was sold on a yield basis little different from that ruling before default. It was evident that the purchaser had not read his daily papers.

The consequences of this collapse spilled over to other securities listed in the same sectors, notably Port of London Authority, but here the security of the stocks was fundamentally different. The PLA stocks could *in extremis* receive support from considerable assets such as valuable property in its territory. Mersey Docks stockholders could look only to the earning power, which had collapsed. We accordingly took a careful look at the PLA stocks, which had been eliminated from our portfolio along with the others. The 3½ per cent stock 1975 had fallen to a level where the yield was about double, or more, the yield on a comparable British government stock. So we bought, feeling that the risk was small and the potential reward large, and in due course the stock was repaid in full on its due date.

Another 'one-off' example of backing a winner was Rolls-Royce debenture stocks. I was in the habit of getting Hansard regularly, and I relied on my secretary to glance through each copy and mark anything that had a bearing on investment. This is a practice I recommend to anyone closely involved in institutional investment. When a receiver had been appointed for Rolls-Royce, as a preliminary to the company's being split into the aero-engine side and the motor-car side, a lengthy statement was made in Parliament. As this filled many columns of Hansard, I took the copy home and read it carefully, more for reasons of general interest than in search of any investment implications.

I formed the view that it was highly probable that the various debenture stocks would be paid in full – and I think any experienced investor carefully reading that Hansard would have come to the same conclusion. I discussed the matter with my colleagues the next day, and as the debenture stocks were quoted at nearly half their face value we decided that this was an opportunity not to be missed.

We thought we might buy a few thousand before the price moved sharply against us, but to our surprise there was an ample supply and within a few weeks we had acquired a substantial six-figure holding. Within about two years we received repayment of capital and arrears of interest in full, reflecting with some puzzlement that the debenture stockholders had benefited far more from receivership than if the company had found a sustained new level of high prosperity.

One might recall here an aphorism of Aneurin Bevan spoken in a different context: 'Why gaze into the crystal when you can read the book?' Fortunately for the London and Manchester, few had 'read the book'.

When Welfare Insurance Company came under the control of London and Manchester Assurance in 1974 we were faced with some very challenging investment problems. The company was in a critical financial position, not because marketable securities were showing heavy depreciation – there were in fact relatively few – but because too much had been placed in doubtful term-mortgages. With the injection of £4,500,000, £2 million cash and £2,500,000 cheap loan money, the problem was to get this money invested before the market took off upwards, which it was about to do. The company's funds were divided into two sections: the various linked contracts, of which the investment trust fund was much the largest, and the general fund. The previous management in its search for liquidity, wherever possible, had sold investment trusts on a massive scale and the investment trust fund was nominally about 90 per cent liquid. As markets had fallen heavily in 1973/4, this move was highly beneficial, but it left the new management with the problem of investing some millions of pounds in investment trust equity stocks – never a free market – with the minimum of delay. We had taken the view that the market was in the early stages of recovery.

One might have been tempted to parcel out this order among a dozen or so brokers in the hope that the wider the cover the better the result. But a large number of brokers all trying to buy investment trust stocks might have given the impression in the market that the demand was even greater than it actually was. So apart from accepting some offers from brokers who happened to have casual selling orders, we gave the main order to the official broker to the fund with instructions that we would take any amounts, however small, of the acceptable companies. It was remarkable how quickly this accumulation in the 'retail' market built up to sizeable amounts. If we had stipulated that only large blocks would be accepted we would have made much slower progress. Of course, it meant more paperwork, and book-keeping, but that was a small price to pay for achieving the strategic objective.

One special device came to our aid. We enquired of Save and Prosper Group if they could supply a large quantity of investment trust units. They happened to have an unusually large book and we bought in one transaction about £750,000 in value. This was not the ideal investment for the linked fund, but it provided a stake in the right specie and gave us time to realize the units as and when we could acquire the particular stocks of our choice. We all breathed a sigh of relief when this exercise was substantially completed.

We had the parallel problem of investing the new money in the general (unlinked) fund. There was no difficulty with the part allocated to gilt-edged, where yields were in double figures. With the equity hypothecation we started buying a carefully selected list of stocks, not among the leaders. The progress was desperately slow because of narrow markets and little supply. One afternoon one of our more far-sighted brokers gave his opinion that the forthcoming trade returns would be much better than expected and that if so the market, already short of stock, could rise substantially. We hurriedly changed our tactics from trying to buy the stocks we particularly wanted, but could not buy, to buying those which were not our first choice, but which we could buy. We selected about twenty stocks, mostly leaders, and gave instructions to put about £25,000 in each. The order, placed mostly with one broker, was completed in a day, without noticeably moving the market – and again we breathed a sigh of relief.

This was the only time I have been on the threshold of a buyer's panic; near enough, at any rate, to realize that it could be even more agonizing than to be involved in a forced liquidation. If one has to buy and misses the market on the way up, one is left with the anguish of having to decide whether to buy at the higher level, thus admitting a past error of judgement, or to wait for a setback with the risk that a second chance does not always occur.

There is one particular investment worth mentioning because of some wider implications. That was the purchase of a substantial holding of Fairview Estates Ltd ordinary shares. In the normal course of business London and Manchester Assurance had an investment in this company of a conventional size, worth about £25,000. When we studied the annual report and accounts in 1975 we became convinced that the outlook was outstandingly promising and that the shares were then very cheap. There was, however, one major snag. Some two million shares (then quoted at about 50p) were owned by a secondary bank currently under the support of the so-called 'lifeboat'. Any distressed sale of these shares could have a disastrous effect on the share price; so we conceived the idea of making a bid for this large holding, hopefully thinking that they could be obtained below the market price.

We took one of our leading broker friends, Freddie Bodem of Henderson Crosthwaite & Co., into our confidence. He was first asked to enquire of the owners whether they might be willing to sell. The answer was encouraging, and we were put in touch with Fairview's chairman, Denis Cope. Bodem and I spent a few hours with Cope and some of his colleagues at the company's head office in Enfield. We came away satisfied, and I submitted the proposition to my board a few days later. While there was general approval in principle, some of my colleagues thought the amount much too large, and accordingly the risk too high. After a lengthy debate it was agreed to bid for half the holding. As it was essential that the whole holding of two million shares should be placed, the brokers set to work to find other buyers for the balance. They succeeded, though not without difficulty, and the deal went through fractionally under the market price, at about 48p.

We then sat back, untroubled, to enjoy what we thought would be a profitable investment. In due course these hopes were amply fulfilled, and at the time of writing the market price is over six times the purchase price. But within a few months of the purchase grave worries appeared. Partly because of general weakness in markets and doubts in particular about Fairview itself, the price started falling rapidly: first to under 40p, then through 30p, and even through 20p, before the tide turned and a recovery took place, almost as quickly as had the fall. I was told that some of the other participants in the placing had become severely rattled, and one gave instructions to 'sell at best', to get out at any price.

It was an unpleasant experience for London and Manchester Assurance, though we could not believe that anything was wrong with Fairview. In course of time one observation became apparent. When my board thought at the time that by reducing the potential commitment to one-half they would be reducing the exposure to risk, the result in the event was precisely the opposite. If the whole amount of about two million shares had been taken by the company, there would have been no weak, anxious holders and the drastic temporary collapse in price would probably never have taken place. I doubt if there is any profound lesson to be learned from this beyond accepting that in most investment matters the unexpected can often happen.

Another interesting question is whether by talking as we did with the chairman of Fairview and his colleagues we would have been guilty of offences under subsequent legislation against 'insider dealing'. I discussed this point with Cope when I met him again recently, and we agreed that at the meeting in question no 'inside' information was in fact given. What Bodem and I learned was probably the most important thing of all, namely, the quality of the people running the company, which could often be discovered without touching upon company affairs at all. If that knowledge constitutes 'insider' information, then every director will have to go into purdah at the approach of a potential shareholder.

Investment Trust Companies

I have already mentioned my fascination with investment trusts, so I am delighted to have had the opportunity of serving on the boards of two of them: Broadstone Investment Trust Ltd (1953–78) and London Trust Ltd (1959–63). Broadstone started life in 1928 as British & German Trust Ltd, formed to specialize in German securities as well as the conventional type of British or North American securities. Its foundation was in the era of the Locarno Treaty: Brüning and Stresemann were in power in Germany, with the hope of a peaceful reconstruction of Europe. This hope was nearly fulfilled, before the advent of Hitler. The outbreak of war made all German investments valueless for the duration; the two preference issues fell heavily into arrears and the asset value of the ordinary stock was negative. The quotation of the ordinary could not likewise be negative; for some years it fluctuated in low single figures and ultimately proved to be one of the best bargains on the whole of the Stock Exchange. The war prompted a change of name and the company was renamed Broadstone Investment Trust Ltd in 1939.

When I came on the scene in 1953, first in the probationary role of investment adviser, the trust was struggling to resuscitate its fortunes with its German interests, all these interests being in the hands of the Custodian of Enemy Property. It was a miracle in my eyes to watch how these 'worthless' German securities acquired some value, whether in West or East Germany, nurtured by some very skilful agents on the spot. By the end of the 1950s all German securities had been realized and the trust became more orthodox, investing predominantly in Great Britain and North America though with one significant difference: it was more ready than most trusts to take a stake in unlisted companies. Largely because of the lack of a quotation and the inability to sell at short notice, they were chosen with extra care, and I believe their performance was on the whole much better than the quoted stocks. The benefit came either through a market quotation on good terms or by a take-over. Two which I remember well were Commercial Plastics, taken over by Courtaulds, and IBM (UK) Ltd before it was absorbed into IBM. It is a pity that more investment trust companies do not encourage the acquisition of unlisted companies. It requires a different expertise from that needed for investing in quoted securities, but it can be very profitable and adds more meaning to the very existence of investment trusts.

Broadstone was managed by Helbert Wagg & Co. Ltd, later merged to form J. H. Schroder Wagg & Co. Ltd. The chairman of Broadstone when I joined was Albert Palache. He was of Dutch origin, and made a special niche for himself in economic history by sponsoring the foundation of sugar beet companies in Great Britain, which later were merged into the British Sugar Corporation. The motive was to save the import of sugar cane in time of war. The venture was a resounding success, helped later by the Common Market, which few if any could have foreseen in the 1930s.

Palache was ably assisted by his deputy, H. E. Netherclift – 'Nether' to all his friends. Although guided by the corporate expertise of Helbert Wagg, both had that wonderful sixth sense which puts a premium on all their investment decisions; and so, more often than not, Broadstone 'beat the averages'. Arrears in the preference stocks were made good and dividends on the ordinary stock were resumed after an interval of many years.

London Trust was independent of any merchant bank and was run by its board and its own management working in harness. It is pointless to attempt to judge which is the better system – management by a merchant bank or independence. Both have advantages, and the crucial test is the quality of the individuals chiefly concerned. London Trust had a wholly orthodox list of investments, though with a strong preference for the financial sectors. By 1982 it had announced the acquisition of several substantial holdings in unlisted and lesser-known quoted companies. This obviously involves more careful selection and adds further justification to the concept of the investment trust.

When I joined these two trust companies the measure of success was almost entirely judged by the asset value of the ordinary capital. Revenue and dividends were deemed to be of secondary importance. Indeed the two, capital and income, were often thought to be in conflict, with the fiction that capital growth was usually found best in low-yielding equities. Gradually the emphasis changed, and income and dividends grew in importance. By the end of the 1970s several trusts were publicizing with pride that revenue and dividends had grown in recent years at rates in excess of the rate of inflation. This alone should justify a high price/earnings multiple – high enough to eliminate the discount between market value and asset value. But large discounts were still prevalent, due mainly to the supply's being greater than the demand. This was aggravated by the flood of new issues by way of rights – several hundred millions – following the halving of the rate of Capital Gains Tax for investment trusts in the budget of 1973. It has since been abolished altogether. With the benefit of hindsight, I feel that large holders of investment trust stocks should have hesitated to sanction the resolutions to increase the capital – but nearly all were passed 'on the nod'.

Much discussion has been taking place about ways and means of reducing the discounts, and some progress has already been made. Some trusts have been taken over completely either by large pension funds or by trading companies, using the device as a means of raising fresh capital, thus reducing the supply. A few have turned themselves into unit trusts. Legislation has been announced which will enable companies, including investment trusts, to use their revenue reserves to buy in their own equity capital. This facility should help to prevent any very large discount. In the USA, where purchase by companies of their own shares has been allowed for very many years, action has been pursued to the point that most trusts (closed-end) have become unit trusts (mutual funds) and the once popular closed-end trust has virtually disappeared.

I have thought for several years that the best solution was somehow to attack the built-in system of perpetual franchise – for in practice no one challenges the re-election of a director, however disappointing he may have proved to be. This objective could be achieved by making it mandatory – by resolution of shareholders – to wind up before some future specified date, unless within a prescribed period the majority of equity shareholders voted to continue for a further extended term. This should ensure that only the best would survive. Boards and managements are reluctant to initiate such a move ('Why should we put our heads on the block?'). However, it would be refreshing if some large shareholder initiated the proposal, which would surely be accepted overwhelmingly by most other shareholders.

In the spring of 1983 London and Manchester Assurance, by virtue of its large holdings of investment trust equities, prompted proposals for conversion into unit trusts. Some of the boards accepted and are implementing such proposals; others are resisting. A successful unitization immediately removes the discount, often about 25 per cent, and results in a material rise in the market price of the investment trust equity. The advantages to the shareholder are so apparent that the logical expectation is for a continuation of this trend. From the point of view of the direction and management, the choice of the portfolio is virtually the same whether investment trust or unit trust, though a different technique is needed to maintain a satisfactory number of units in issue.

In one way or another the supply of investment trust equities is likely to decrease while the demand should grow no less. The inherent advantages remain, and I am still convinced that there are few better and more worry-free long-term investments than well-managed investment trust equity stocks or shares.

Professional Advice

Throughout my time with Equity and Law, London and Manchester Assurance and Welfare Insurance, I was deeply grateful for the skilled advice and kindly interest of many stockbroking firms. Those we got to know well were taken into our confidence and our problems and objectives were adequately explained. I can recall no occasion of such confidence being abused. We endeavoured to give speedy replies to any recommendation, partly from courtesy but also from enlightened self-interest. A broker with a good recommendation or an appealing bid or offer is prone to go to the client who will give him the quickest reply. Those who are slow to respond, or who do not even answer at all, cannot complain if they go to the bottom of the list.

Booms and Slumps

I have never attempted to count the number of cyclical booms and depressions, or bull markets and bear markets, that I have witnessed. There must have been at least half a dozen major ones in my business life. I have not read any rational explanation of why these cycles occur, or why the shares of companies with an almost unbroken record of past growth, combined with confident expectations of future growth, do not rise in a nearly straight line upwards – but these cycles have occurred ever since stock markets began and no doubt will continue indefinitely. There may be special reasons for the start and end of each cycle, but they all have certain common features.

Usually, prices fall faster than they rise. This may be because fear provokes a quicker reaction than hope. A pleasant corollary, however, is that bull markets last longer than bear markets. It is axiomatic that the peak of a bull market is accompanied by the greatest optimism and the trough of a bear market by the deepest pessimism. It follows, therefore, that the investor who hopes to buy near the bottom and sell near the top must be prepared to swim against the tide. But where are the signs that the tide is about to turn? There is one which I have found – if one can detect it – that is more reliable than most. It is when, in a bear market, prices no longer fall on bad news, or in a bull market no longer go up on good news; in short, when bad or good news is fully discounted in prices.

On a practical level, I have found that committees of a few people can often be very good at buying at low prices, for statistics can usually reinforce the argument. Committees, however, are usually bad at selling near the top. In the surrounding aura of optimism the argument is too often: 'Why sell a good share when the outlook looks promising?' I believe a single person in authority, with plenty of courage is more likely to sell at the right time. Strangely, selling good shares at high prices requires more courage than buying at low prices. I remember being told by a City editor of a popular newspaper that if he recommended a share that went down in price all was forgiven, but if he recommended a sale and the price went up then he was 'in the dock, on a near-criminal charge'.

To See or Not to See

Many investors, professional and amateur, have at times been lured by the bait that they can learn more of their investment by visual inspection: and I relate my own experiences – and the lessons learned – in this particular field.

I was an original shareholder in the Great Universal Stores which was issued on a prospectus in 1931. If I had held on to my modest investment of £100 it would have been worth about £225,000 today. Not long after the issue the shares went to a worrying discount, which seems incredible to those accustomed to seeing a succession of record profits year after year. There was no satisfactory explanation for this temporary collapse, so rather than do nothing I took a bus one Saturday afternoon to look at the only property I could identify from the prospectus – a warehouse in Hackney. All I could see was a large building with the name of the company plainly visible, but nothing else: it was a waste of the bus fare. I think I sold my shares when the price recovered to around its issue price.

On my various visits to the United States I used to make a habit of looking into a Woolworth store – not because my company had invested in Woolworths but as a matter of general interest. Time after time this lacklustre business showed no signs of visible improvement until on my last visit I thought I detected a marked change for the better, but paradoxically the amount of customers seemed to have diminished materially.

In this country many people shopping in, say, Boots, Marks & Spencer or Sainsburys are impressed by the quality and good value of the merchandise, but unless they are experts they cannot possibly form a judgement on the all-important profit margins. So usually investors in retail trade companies can expect to learn little of value by just looking. Occasionally, there are exceptions. The phenomenal success of the recent issue of Superdrug shares was due, I think, to many investors having seen and been favourably impressed by a typical store in their neighbourhood.

Sponsored or guided tours of factories can be rewarding. When Equity and Law was asked to underwrite the whole of a moderate issue of preference capital in a high technology machine tool company in the Midlands, I was taken on a tour of the factory and learned much more than figures could convey. On another occasion I was given the opportunity of visiting in New England the American subsidiary of a British textile combine where Equity and Law had an investment. The vice-president in charge made a fetish of touching and examining cloth in various stages of processing, but he never spoke once to any of his employees, which obviously created an unfavourable impression.

On the whole, I think the wise rule is to be wary of expecting to learn much that is worth while from an investor's viewpoint by a casual inspection of physical assets – unless one is an expert in the field under review. The pitfalls can be as numerous as the rewards.

Miscellany

During my long sojourn on the investment scene, I met a number of incidents, either amusing or off-the-beaten-track, which have stayed fresh in my memory, and which I now pass on.

During the war, in 1942/3, when relations with Russia were better than for many years, there was some speculative interest in Imperial Russian bonds, which were then quoted about 2 or 3 per cent, instead of, as previously, being completely worthless. Equity and Law owned a few, and we decided to sell and realize the few hundred pounds they could fetch. But there was one holding which apparently had not been stamped and was accordingly not good delivery. We left the scrip with the brokers in the hope that some day the market price would exceed the cost of the stamp.

A few years later, in 1948 I think, the brokers telephoned to say that they had installed new lighting in their office and happened to re-examine these Russian bonds. They discovered an embossed stamp, just visible, and the bonds were thus good delivery. We instructed them to sell if possible at any price, and they got about the same as the earlier sales in 1942/3. As the 'cold war' had intensified we enquired how anyone could possibly be interested. The answer was that there was a strong demand from lampshade manufacturers, who valued the fine parchment. Here was one exception to the tag: 'It's not worth the paper it's written on.'

An elderly colleague told me a delightful tale of a meeting of trustees of a charitable trust in Scotland, who had assembled to review the trust's investments. One of these was Niger Company 5 per cent debenture stock. A trustee enquired if the company had formerly had anything to do with the slave trade, and how it was currently treating the natives. When the answer was not wholly to his satisfaction he insisted that the stock should be sold, but added: 'Don't take a penny less than 95'. A nice mixture of conscience and parsimony!

My first introduction to Alfred Herbert Ltd as an investment makes rueful reading in the light of the company's recent troubles. Shortly after the end of the war, when I was at Equity and Law, we were offered a block of 10,000 shares at just under £5. The shares were not officially quoted but were dealt in under what was then the equivalent of Rule 163. The balance sheet and recent record were outstandingly good. Net liquid assets were about the equivalent of the price offered, and we willingly accepted the offer. Some few years later we heard that the share had changed hands at about £11, which naturally pleased us. Soon afterwards, however, to our great surprise, the dividend was savagely cut without any indication of changed fortunes. We asked the brokers if they could explain, and they replied that they thought the elderly founding father, with his mind on death duties, was so angry at the big jump in the (unofficial) price that he expressed his displeasure in this unusual way. Many companies have paid or increased their dividends without real justification, but this was the only case I met of the opposite.

During the war I witnessed an unusual instance of benefiting from 'mistaken identity'. When the Japanese were overrunning South-East Asia, any investment in that area suffered badly – especially those in Malaya. There was a rubber company, Malayalam, which fell in price acutely, due to its alleged connection with Malaya. An astute broker drew this company to our attention, and pointed out that it operated in India, far away from the fighting. It was a good company, and a purchase was strongly recommended. We acted on this advice – and later benefited from it.

We are accustomed now to all British government stocks being free of Capital Gains Tax, if held for over a year, and it is easy to forget that in the early days of this tax only those stocks issued after a certain date were exempt. This led to one particular absurdity. Two separate *tranches* of one particular stock were issued in satisfaction of industries being nationalized. The stocks were similar in all material aspects except that, having been issued at different times, one was subject to Capital Gains Tax, the other was exempt. When the difference was first explained in the House of Commons my colleague Nigel Birch aptly described the victims of this difference as 'spotted dogs'.

As time went on the difference, some liable, some exempt, was becoming more and more confusing and illogical, and one day, when I was working for London and Manchester Assurance, the investment manager at the time, William White, suggested that it would be wise to concentrate our holding of British government stocks in those most likely to benefit from the spots being taken off the dogs. The best candidate was 3 per cent Transport Stock 1978/88, then about 50 and then liable for Capital Gains Tax. This stock soon became our largest holding. It not only proved very profitable, but it soon became a yardstick for measuring other investments, in particular equities as a group. We often used to work out where the FT 30-share index would have to be in 1988 to do better as regards capital than the 3 per cent stock 1978/88 with its freedom from Capital Gains Tax. This comparison is still a useful exercise. (To illustrate this point with autumn 1983 prices, the FT 30-share index at 700 would have to reach 999 in 1988 to do better than 3 per cent Transport Stock 1978/88 at around 77 – quite a tall order!)

What Makes a Successful Investor?

In a chapter on investment it is cowardly not to attempt an answer to this question. The first requirement is to be clear about your objective. Is the aim the highest income consistent with safety? Is capital appreciation the primary objective? How much risk are you prepared to run?

The next step is to be as well informed as possible about the relevant facts. This involves a careful reading of financial columns in daily papers and journals and company reports, including the auditor's report. Attendance at company annual general meetings can often be informative – even if only routine.

The rest is judgement, intrinsic and comparative, as you are always backing your judgement against all the others who make the market. Usually, the highest reward comes from swimming against the tide, which requires courage when buying and lack of greed when selling. Obviously one wants to seek the best advice possible, which usually means choosing a stockbroker in whom you have full confidence and informing him of your circumstances and objectives.

Luck is an ever-present ingredient. I have never forgotten some words I heard several years ago at a Trafalgar Night dinner at Portsmouth. The admiral who was proposing the toast to the immortal memory spoke of Nelson's 'contriving to make luck his ally'. The successful investor should attempt likewise. It is not impossible. Many experienced investors have been able to sense when luck is running for or against them, and act accordingly. In any case, it is good discipline to question whether the profitable outcome of an investment is due to skill or luck. A combination of both is the ideal.

Unfortunately, the successful investor must always pay careful attention to the incidence of Capital Gains Tax. Full use and careful phasing should be made of the annual personal allowance. Also, any British government stock showing a material loss within a year of purchase should be switched into the nearest comparable stock.

Finally, most successful investors have been patient.

I cannot conclude this chapter on investment without recording my profound admiration for the skill and integrity of the best stockbroking firms – and indeed for the City as a whole. The Stock Exchange certainly lives up to its motto, freely translated as: 'My word is my bond'. The City and its institutions benefit from the compactness of the 'Square Mile' and from their practice of transacting nearly all their business in the first instance by the spoken word. This is only possible if a high degree of trust is present, which is so now and, I confidently believe, will remain so.

CHAPTER 4
Passing Interludes

In mid-career I had some occupations – and the possibility of others – away from the mainstream of my activities, all influenced, directly or indirectly, by Lord Piercy. I met him first in 1940, when he was still William Piercy, partner in the firm of stockbrokers acting for Bank Insurance Trust Corporation Ltd, controlled by Equity and Law Life Assurance Society. I had had an earlier contact with this unit trust group in my stockbroking days shortly before the outbreak of war. In the endeavour to hasten the slow-moving progress of unit trusts, the managers conceived the idea of a dual-capital trust. Cornhill Trust (of Bank and Insurance shares) was formed, part in the form of a 4 per cent fifteen-year debenture, guaranteed as to capital and interest by Equity and Law, and part in deferred units. Although Buckmaster & Moore was not then favourably inclined to unit trusts, the Cornhill debentures, issued at a small discount, looked so cheap that the firm recommended them strongly and placed a large part of the total issue of some £1,500,000. What was not publicly known at the time was what happened, on the other side of the coin, to the necessary amount of the deferred units. They were a marginal, highly geared and low-yielding investment, not ideal in a time of threatening war.

When I moved to Equity and Law in the spring of 1940 I

found that the greater part of the deferred had been taken by the society, an investment of, I think, some £750,000. By the summer of 1940 these units had fallen from the issue price of about fifteen shillings to only a few shillings – almost option money. The managers wanted to issue more deferred units to restore a proper balance between the market values of the two classes – and the small print of the trust deed allowed this to be done. My actuarial friends at Equity and Law were able to demonstrate that as the price of the deferred fell near to zero an enormous quantity of new deferred units could legally be issued, thus diluting the specie to such an extent that recovery to the price paid by the original investors was virtually impossible.

Steps were accordingly taken, by persuasion, to prevent the issue of further deferred, and I remember that Piercy was particularly helpful in his capacity as broker to the managers in persuading them to accept the logic of this complicated situation.

By the end of the war it had not been too difficult to bring about a vast improvement in the investments of Equity and Law; but one intractable problem remained with the holding of Cornhill deferred. They could not be realized by selling the underlying securities in the trust, and there was no demand for them by new investors. The only way of realizing them was to be able to surrender to the managers the appropriate amount of the debentures, and the combined package was eligible for liquidation by selling the underlying securities in the trust. The society therefore had to tempt holders of the debenture by offering a premium over their market value and then offer the combined package for liquidation. In this way the unduly large holding of Cornhill deferred units was ultimately realized on reasonable terms, though only over a period of painstaking work lasting several months.

I had become familiar with many aspects of unit trusts, and with the encouragement of Equity and Law I was appointed to the board of Bank Insurance Trust Corporation, later renamed Save and Prosper Group. I took an increasingly active part in the group and retired as deputy chairman in 1961. Although Piercy was soon to move to new spheres of activity – Lord Piercy, director of the Bank of England and first chairman of Industrial and Commercial Finance Corporation – he still retained a keen interest in unit trusts. Together, we submitted a joint paper on unit trusts to Sir Ronald Edwards' well-known seminar at the London School of Economics.

When I had decided to leave Equity and Law in 1952 to seek 'fresh woods, and pastures new', I confided in Piercy and sought his help and advice. At our first meeting, he said: 'How about steel?' The Conservatives had recently returned to power and were pledged to denationalize steel. I replied immediately that I would be keenly interested, though I did not have any very high hopes. At our next meeting he said that he had given my name to the authorities, and added: 'The penny dropped.' The 'penny' could not have looked very valuable in the eyes of the authorities, as I heard nothing more. However, I was beginning to get re-established with an appointment to the boards of London and Manchester Assurance and also Associated Equipment Company, in addition to my continuing work with Bank Insurance Trust Corporation.

Piercy did not give up easily, and in his kindness was determined to help me. Industrial and Commercial Finance Corporation (ICFC) had a minority holding in a small hire purchase finance company, Mutual Finance, whose chairman was the Earl of Limerick, a director of ICFC. At Piercy's suggestion I was invited to join the board of Mutual Finance. The invitation was given over the telephone by Lord Limerick, with arrangements to meet at an early date. Before the meeting could take place, Thos. Tilling made a successful bid for the whole of Mutual Finance, so that opening door was shut.

However, not long afterwards, in 1955, I was appointed to the board of ICFC. The company had been formed in 1945 largely to fill what had become known as the 'Macmillan gap'. The Macmillan Report, drawn up under the chairmanship of Lord Macmillan, a Scottish law lord, and published in 1931, had exposed the difficulty of finding capital for small businesses requiring up to £200,000. The shareholders of ICFC were the Bank of England and the English and Scottish clearing banks, which provided the loan finance and nominated the directors. The representative of Lloyds Bank, Hugh Roberts, had recently died, and I was appointed to fill the vacancy. Apparently Piercy must have convinced Lloyds Bank that I was suitable, as I was never interviewed by the bank. Some years later I was acknowledged in a charming manner by the chairman of Lloyds Bank, Sir Oliver Franks, now Lord Franks.

The concept of ICFC sounded good in theory, and I soon found that it worked even better in practice. Piercy and his general manager, John Kinross, worked in harness and all submissions to the board were well prepared and convincingly explained. The non-executive directors covered a wide range of business experience. Although I cannot remember any recommendation's being refused, the board members were certainly not 'yes-men', and at times minor modifications were made. On the very few occasions when any issue of substance arose the custom was to discuss it afterwards in the chairman's room, reporting later to the full board if appropriate. This, I think, is a good practice and can sometimes avoid unnecessary argument across the board table.

The results of ICFC in its formative years showed a rising trend of profit and loss account, due in no small way to the willingness to take a minority share of the equity of its borrowers. Of course, some of its loans became 'doubtful' and provisions had to be made, but these provisions were usually more than offset by the success of the equity

91

investments. The more notable of the latter included Thorn Electrical Industries, now part of Thorn-EMI; Marchon Products, now part of Albright & Wilson; and Sir George Godfrey & Partners, which specialized in the air-pressurization of aircraft.

Shortly after I joined the board, the management hierarchy was strengthened by the engagement of Gordon Richardson, now Lord Richardson, KG, and recently Governor of the Bank of England. Before coming to ICFC he had made a great name at the Bar, and I remember well being fascinated by the barrister's skill, and his in particular, of explaining the most complicated problem in simple language so that the listeners could grasp the salient points without difficulty. Meeting regularly at least once a month, we got to know each other, and I was sad when he left about two years later to join Schroders as the heir-apparent.

Our paths were soon to cross again. One day when I was in my office at London and Manchester Assurance in Finsbury Square, Gordon telephoned to suggest a meeting, as there was something he wanted to discuss with me. When we met I remember his opening words: 'I don't quite know how to begin,' which on reflection was an unusual preamble for a skilled barrister. He soon came to the point, which was to invite me to join the board of Schroders with a special responsibility for their investment departments. The idea appealed to me immediately and I had further meetings with Gordon and his colleagues, including discussions about the precise nature of the work, which would involve moving my office to Schroders. At that time I had convinced myself that I would accept. I got full encouragment from Lionel Fraser, head of Helbert Wagg & Co. – before they merged with Schroders to form J. H. Schroder Wagg & Co. – who was also chairman of Broadstone Investment Trust. The thought that I might succeed to the chairmanship of London and Manchester Assurance had never entered my head, but my colleagues there had been kind and encouraging, and I thought that a move away from Finsbury Square would be construed as a disloyal act. That consideration made me decide to decline, though many times afterwards I felt I had made a great mistake. I had already some good friends in Schroder's and subsequently made many more. I would undoubtedly have been happy in the work there, and I don't think any conflicts of interest would have arisen. In business life, as in most other respects, one is seldom given a second chance, and I mention this 'might-have-been' in the hope that, if any of my friends in Schroder Wagg read these words, they will be made aware of my regret.

To return again to activities with ICFC, Piercy, while actively engaged in the day-to-day affairs of the corporation, acquired another interest which absorbed much of his time – an active membership of the Kuwait Investment Board. The origin of this board reads like a chapter out of the *Arabian Nights*. Kuwait, not yet a sovereign state, was under the protection of Great Britain, and oil in vast quantities had only recently been discovered. Legend relates that the wise and venerable ruler Sheikh Abdullah al Salim Al Sabah, had a dream, or rather a nightmare, that his oil wells had run dry, and consequently the growing affluence of his subjects would revert to poverty. He then sought the means to provide a 'nest-egg' out of the increasing wealth. The Bank of England was brought into consultation and the investment board was set up in the City of London to invest the balance of oil royalties as safely and profitably as possible.

A public announcement was made and the first members of the board were: Mr Kemp, the Ruler's representative in the UK; Charles Whishaw, now Sir Charles, partner in Freshfields, solicitors; Lord Kennet of the Dene, whom I had known as a director of Equity and Law Life Assurance; and Lord Piercy. All investments were registered in Bank of England nominees and stockbrokers and others involved in the operations were pledged to secrecy. The day-to-day work was done by Piercy and reported regularly to the full board. General guidance and sanction was given by the Ruler and his advisers, particularly on such matters as the percentage allowed in equities. This percentage started at a low figure and was raised from time to time, encouraged by the rising trend in the market. Not long after the formation of this board I was invited, with the consent of the Ruler and the Bank of England, to join it in 1959. Piercy and I used to meet frequently in his room and go through the portfolio. Fortunately, our ideas on the general strategy were usually in agreement and we had advice from a panel of leading stockbrokers – and always a weighty consultation with the government broker on all matters relating to gilt-edged securities. After about a year on the board I was invited to accompany Piercy on one of his visits to Kuwait.

We flew in a Britannia (BOAC) aircraft, calling at Rome and Damascus. When touching down at Damascus I could see the perimeter of the airfield ringed with several dozen anti-aircraft guns, though no gunners were in sight. Syria was then 'federated' with Egypt. In Kuwait we were lodged in the Government Hospitality House, and the next day had an audience with the Ruler. Any weighty investment matter was reserved for a meeting with the Finance Minister and the conversation, through an interpreter, was confined to an exchange of courtesies. There was, however, one financial matter which cropped up. Kuwait was about to start its own currency, having been linked up to then to the Indian rupee. The Ruler asked Piercy if he thought it a good idea to make the paper note as large as possible in the hope that people might think it more valuable than a smaller note. In diplomatic language Piercy replied that the quality of the paper might be more significant than its size.

Later in our brief visit we had a meeting with the Finance Minister accompanied by one of those ubiquitous Scotsmen, by the name of McGregor, who have a habit of filling such roles throughout the world. I believe the percentage in equities was discussed, and I cannot remember any difficulty in getting this increased when requested. This is unlike a similar restriction, which I observed, in the limits placed on equity investments of life assurance companies in the United States. Most are restricted to state legislation, and some of my American friends had told me that only in boom conditions could they get the state legislatures to alter the laws to allow an increase. No public criticism can be expected in such circumstances, though from the life assurance point of view the right time to allow an increase is in a slump, when prices are low. Sadly, legislators seldom think that way. When the first major revision of the British Trustees Act was made in 1961 to allow an element of equities, it happened at a time of a temporary boom.

There was one other matter of general guidance which the board had to observe. The Kuwaiti authorities had a dislike of local authority stocks, whether they be London, Liverpool or Bradford. We had accordingly to dispose of a substantial holding of a short-dated LCC loan. In the light of all that has happened since, perhaps the Kuwaiti authorities were more far-sighted than their advisers in the City of London.

The Kuwait Oil Company people showed us over their installations and refineries: a case of 'oil, oil, everywhere, and not a drop to see'. One of the things that I remember well and which impressed me most was their training school. Bedouin youths were recruited from the desert and, largely by blackboard instruction, were taught first simple, and later quite complicated operations – and the instructors spoke very highly of their ability.

One evening we were entertained by the Finance Minister to a banquet. The table was as large as the mown part of a cricket pitch. All comestibles were laid out at the same time on large plates on the table. There must have been about forty or fifty guests, including ladies. My neighbour, Mrs

McGregor, was asked by an Arab waiter what she wanted, and she pointed to an appetizing plate of carved pieces of cold lamb. The waiter served her politely with the help of a spoon and fork, and then asked me what my choice was. I pointed to the same dish and a large hand grabbed an ample portion and put it on my plate though, mercifully, I was given a fork to eat it with. There was, of course, no alcohol, only Coca-Cola and the like, and goats' milk; but Piercy and I had been suitably fortified beforehand and at the McGregor home. Among the guests was a party of senior people from Shell. Unlike us, they had flown out from England on a chartered aeroplane. The pilot apparently had not known the rule that prior notification of a non-scheduled flight was necessary, at any rate with the Syrian authorities. When the plane reached Syrian air-space some angry Syrian fighters buzzed it and forced it to land. After some altercation the Shell party was allowed to proceed and told not to do it again.

On our return to England the management of this rapidly growing fund proceeded much as before, though soon a full-time investment manager was appointed – Bruce Dawson, recruited from the investment department of Standard Life Assurance in Edinburgh. A fair measure of autonomy was allowed to this London–based board, but Kuwaiti practices soon became more noticeable. The first one to note was in connection with the reception held on the Kuwait national day, and to which the investment board members were invited. The custom had been to receive several hundred guests in a large London hotel and refresh them with ample offerings of champagne. Then one year the edict went out that Muslim laws must be obeyed and no alcohol served. The large number of guests arrived to be offered many kinds of drinks – all soft. I like to think that most of my fellow British guests stayed the allotted time, but certainly the decibels of conversation recorded a lower figure.

The second major Kuwaiti influence on us was the grow-ing importance of the Arab ban on all commerce with Israel. This was extended to the investment portfolio and anything with an Israeli connection (e.g. Marks & Spencer, Great Universal Stores, J. Lyons & Co) was proscribed. It soon became more personal. I do not think we had invested in the shares of the Leyland Motor Corporation, but it was noted that Leyland had a thriving assembly plant at Ashdod in Israel, and that I was a director of Leyland. I do not know who did the prompting, but the message got through that I was no longer *persona grata* and a date was fixed for my departure. I felt very unhappy about this. I had not been involved in the age-long conflict between Jew and Arab and I thought I was doing a useful job of work. As the date of departure approached the Kuwaiti authorities must have started thinking about the old adage: 'Better the devil you know than the devil you don't.' A message was sent to me through the Ambassador (Kuwait having become a sovereign state): if I chose to disclose my remuneration from Leyland then Kuwait would pay me the same or more, provided I resigned from Leyland. I did not need any time to consider my reply. My first loyalty was to Leyland, and I declined this unusual proposal.

We parted, however, on the most friendly terms. I was asked to suggest the names of one or two people to take my place, and Mervyn Talbot-Rice, a chartered accountant and a director of investment trusts, and Ian Henderson, a former stockbroker and also a director of investment trusts, were appointed to the board. Sadly, Mervyn died not long after his appointment. Another gesture of parting goodwill was the request to prepare a paper for a forthcoming meet-ing of OPEC states setting out my considered opinion of the comparative merits of the shares of oil companies quoted in Britain and the shares of companies in the finan-cial sectors, especially insurance.

I enlisted the help of Nicholas Davenport of L. Messel

and Co., stockbrokers, who had a good reputation as experts on oil shares. We were able to produce sound arguments in favour of insurance and bank shares, and subsequent events have justified this view. Thus I like to think that as I bowed out of this fascinating interlude in my career and was able to devote more time to my mainstream activities with life assurance, I may have left in the archives of some oil-rich state in the Middle East a vote of confidence in the integrity, efficiency and prosperity of British insurance.

CHAPTER 5
The Motor Industry

The origin of my involvement with the motor industry arose by chance, and was in no sense premeditated. An elderly friend, and client in my stockbroking days, Sir Frederick Sykes, used to call on me from time to time at my office in Lincoln's Inn Fields, when I was working for Equity and Law Life Assurance, usually to talk about investment matters. On one such occasion in early 1953, he said he might be able to 'influence a directorship your way', and asked if I would be interested. I replied that I had decided to leave Equity and Law at the next annual general meeting in April, and that I would be greatly interested. He did not disclose the name of the company, but as he was a director of two investment trusts in addition to some industrial interests I assumed it would be one of the former.

A few months later he told me that everything had been arranged and I then enquired, trying to conceal my acute interest, the name of the company, 'AEC,' he replied, adding: 'I am chairman.' Now, I knew nothing about making buses or trucks, though I could probably understand their financial results. I readily accepted, hoping that, in some way beyond my imagination at the time, this connection might turn out to mutual advantage. Thus began an involvement with the motor industry which was to last nearly twenty years, through various stages and always as a non-executive director.

I took up my duties in April 1953 and regularly attended monthly board meetings, usually in Berkeley Square and sometimes at the factory at Southall – alas, now razed to the ground for redevelopment. Associated Equipment Company, which in the earlier days was part of the Underground Electric Railways of London (later London Passenger Transport Board), was the largest company in the Associated Commercial Vehicles group. While it proudly displayed on its factory walls the slogan 'Makers of London buses', it made only the chassis, which on completion usually went to Park Royal Vehicles to have the body, whether single-deck or double-deck, added. The controlling group owned a separate sales company, ACV Sales, whose job was to seek out orders which were passed on where appropriate to AEC, which carried them out and invoiced the product to ACV Sales at cost, plus a fixed percentage for profit – a legacy of the LPTB days. In theory this meant that the higher the cost of production at AEC, the greater the profit to that company. I don't think the system was ever abused and costs deliberately inflated, but it seemed to me fundamentally wrong in principle.

The monthly board meetings consisted mainly of reports by the principal executives, made verbally with supporting papers; followed by questions and answers. I do not recollect any major policy matter ever being debated. That was the province of the controlling company. While I found the work interesting and enjoyed the company of my new colleagues, I soon came to the conclusion that there was little scope for a non-executive director.

I accordingly sought a meeting with C. W. Reeve, the *de facto* chief executive of the group, though he was officially designated finance director. I told him my views and that I was reconciled to the idea of leaving. He accepted the general conclusion, but added that I should not lose heart and feel there was no useful function. Some day, something unexpected might happen which would justify my role. I was glad to accept his advice and decided to soldier on.

I gradually got to know other people in the group, in particular Herbert Hill, a non-executive director of Park Royal Vehicles, whose main work was as head of the Birfield Industries, a very flourishing component firm, sold several years later to GKN. We found we shared the same anxieties about the structure of the group, with its debilitating system of 'cost-plus' and, most important, the lack of a strong managing director at group headquarters. We sought a meeting with Lord Brabazon, ACV chairman, with a view to pressing our convictions, even to the point of resignation. Indeed, I had typed out my own letter of resignation, with the reasons, and had it in my pocket.

At this meeting, when I feared I might be told to mind my own particular business, Hill opened with a brilliant and persuasive exposition of our worries, whereupon 'Brab' immediately warmed to us and said, in words to this effect: 'Thank God someone has told me what is wrong with my company.' We then got down to discussing practical remedies, in particular, that W. R. (Bill) Black, later Lord Black, should be appointed group managing director with all the powers normally granted to a chief executive. We were both asked to join the board of ACV, even if that meant giving up our directorships of the two manufacturing companies. We were to form a small committee with Bill Black to decide and recommend to the full board of ACV various courses of action to improve its profitability.

The first moves were obvious. The practice of 'cost-plus' was abolished, along with the mentality which originated it. Every subsidiary company had to stand on its own feet and earn an acceptable profit. Crossley Motors, a bus business in Lancashire, and one of the wholly owned subsidiaries of ACV, had been losing money year after year and was showing no signs of recovery. In spite of strenuous local protests it was closed down, and I believe most of the employees found new work within a few weeks. Maudsley Motors, another subsidiary, made chassis, fire engines, and various specialized products such as dump-trucks. Their factory was in a remote area of the west Midlands, near Alcester, and so far distant from towns that they could attract labour only by paying the bus fares from many workers' homes: a very expensive extra cost. The true cost of assembling chassis was well above that at Southall and was discontinued, leaving the company to concentrate on its specialized products.

The autonomy of the sales company was gradually diminished, allowing the factories to take a closer interest in selling their own products. A rising young star, Jim Slater, who had attracted attention as secretary of Park Royal Vehicles, was given an important group appointment as a commercial director and travelled far and wide in the furtherance of business. The group soon began to function as a well-organized concern backed up by good and skilled engineering – but it could not be made immune from the adversities of periodical trade slumps. One such slump of considerable severity occurred in the late 1950s, and the ordinary dividend was cut from 22½ per cent to 10 per cent. Naturally all the board members were worried and Lord Brabazon, in particular, was searching for a substantial partner, which might stabilize the buffeting. He thought Rolls-Royce might be ideal. It was heavily involved in aero-engines, made a very specialized and expensive car in relatively small quantities, and had not yet fulfilled its highest hopes in diesel engines. The two companies together might add up to more than the sum of their two separate parts.

I happened to know very well at that time the finance director of Rolls-Royce, William Gill. He is my exact contemporary – we were born on the same day. He is a Scottish chartered accountant, and we saw a great deal of each other while we were studying for our respective professions in Glasgow. I was asked to meet him and say that a bid of about £1 over the current price of ACV shares, then around thirty shillings, would probably be acceptable. We duly met for dinner one evening and I did my best to persuade him that ACV was on the path to recovery and was capable of reaching its former prosperity. I did not succeed in this mission, and we learned afterwards that, while Rolls-Royce was not averse to the idea, it did not believe ACV to be capable of the recovery envisaged – which in due course did take place. This flirtation remains one of the more intriguing 'ifs' in the industry. If the marriage had come off, independence from Leyland would probably have been preserved and Rolls-Royce might have been saved from receivership and dismemberment a few years later. But no one should be blamed for not believing a forecast, especially an optimistic one.

While ACV started its new lease of life by shedding loss-making activities, it was by no means in an entirely negative frame of mind. When it learned that Thornycroft (Transport) of Basingstoke and the Solent might be for sale, it acted positively, and after careful investigation and tough negotiations it bought the Basingstoke factory on favourable terms. The advantages were the additional facilities in a different area, where skilled labour was obtainable, and the benefits from the company having recently obtained a large order from the War Office for heavy tank transporters known as the 'Mighty Antar', with the hope in time of using AEC engines.

In the continual search for overseas markets it was realized that South Africa was one of its weakest, while it was one of the best for the arch-rival, Leyland. Drastic action was needed. The local representatives were replaced by taking a controlling interest in J. H. Plane (Africa), a thrusting and efficient organization. Rebates were given to encourage sales and a very shrewd deal was done in purchasing

103

a strategic holding in PUTCO, a bus company mainly concerned with busing non-whites to their places of work. By virtue of this shareholding, with the ability if needed to inject fresh capital, considerable influence was obtained in the placing of orders for buses which went more and more to AEC and less and less to Leyland. As the profit margins were good, ACV benefited considerably and Leyland suffered.

The annual general meetings of ACV were usually held in the Mayfair Hotel. Lord Brabazon always treated them with great respect, and not a little alarm. He never forgot that boards, however successful, were the servants of the shareholders. Each year he gave me the task of thinking of every relevant question which might be asked and then ensuring that there was a correct answer to each. They often numbered two or three dozen, but none was ever asked. If they had been, I am sure he would not have had to refer to the written brief but would have answered from memory.

In the years of gathering strength for ACV – the early 1960s – the shadow of Leyland was seldom absent. Leyland's products were the yardstick by which ours had to be measured: price, power, speed, fuel consumption, and so on. They were a formidable competitor, but Leyland had anxieties of its own, and long before the merger with ACV finally took place, Leyland was thinking hard about acquiring ACV. It missed a great opportunity at the time of the negotiations with Rolls-Royce.

In the early part of 1962 negotiations started in earnest: Sir Henry Spurrier and Donald Stokes on the Leyland side, Lord Brabazon and Bill Black on the ACV side. Leyland's idea was to offer four of its shares for five of ACV's shares, though ACV believed that share-for-share might be accepted. When the news of the negotiations reached the ACV board there was much searching of heart. To bed down with their arch-rival was anathema to many ACV directors, especially the executive directors, who had spent most of their recent years devising every possible means of outwitting Leyland. Leyland shares were then about £4 compared with about £3 for ACV. An offer on a share-for-share basis would bring immediate financial gain to ACV shareholders, and a refusal would require a lot of explaining. I was well aware that a satisfactory explanation of a refusal would be nearly impossible.

During this time of heart-searching I remember going up in the lift with Lord Brabazon to his flat in Rutland Gate, where we often lunched after board meetings. We were alone, and Brab asked me, in very few words: 'This Leyland business, do we say yes or no?' I replied: 'Share-for-share, yes.' He was a man who paid attention to simple, direct answers and had little patience with long-winded explanations. By the time the lift reached his flat I felt he had come to the same conclusion. Events moved with speed and, Leyland realized that share-for-share was the only way to succeed. The boards met one afternoon soon afterwards at their respective offices on opposite sides of Berkeley Square, and recommended the deal. They then met together in the Leyland offices where Brab, as always, rose to the occasion and in graceful words said to the Leyland chairman: 'Henry, up to this morning we were your deadly rivals, now we are your staunchest friends.' And so began a splendid partnership.

But sadly, Sir Henry Spurrier was on the threshold of a mortal illness. Although he was delighted by the merger he was unduly pessimistic about the immediate outlook and was on the point of writing to shareholders warning them of disappointing results ahead with a possible cut in dividend. He was persuaded against doing so, which in the event would have been unjustified and needlessly alarming.

BMC, which had had talks with Leyland earlier, received the news with some dismay.

Spurrier's illness soon progressed to the stage when his successor had to be nominated and appointed, and the choice fell on Black. No better choice could have been made. Then Sir William Black, he was immensely knowledgeable about the industry – he had received one of the highest accolades in 1953 when he was president of the Society of Motor Manufacturers and Traders – he was shrewd, diplomatic, very just, well liked and had a delightful sense of humour. He guided the new, enlarged Leyland with skill and success, ably supported by his managing director, Donald Stokes.

In the meantime, ACV continued as a separate company, though a wholly owned subsidiary, and held regular board meetings as formerly. I continued on the board but all major decisions were taken by the parent, Leyland, and I felt as if I were back in the old AEC days – with nominal responsibility but little influence. This did not last long, as in 1966 I was appointed to the board of the Leyland Motor Corporation, which delighted me greatly. I looked forward to becoming familiar with the prestigious works at Leyland, in Lancashire.

The company had a reputation for paternalism, which was easily detected even on the first visit. But it was of the beneficial kind. Everyone was encouraged to feel proud of the company. The bosses looked after the interests of their workers, and as a rule won their respect. The company trained its apprentices well and made a great occasion of their annual prize-giving, when parents and relatives joined the audience in the large assembly hall. On this occasion awards were also given to winners under the 'suggestion' scheme. These awards were no mean token prizes of £25 or £50. They were often several hundred pounds, and were sometimes in the thousands. They were designed to bear a direct relation to the benefit to the company of the employee's suggestion. The existence of a suggestion scheme, with realistic awards, is a powerful stimulus and incentive as well as an antidote to boredom, especially in repetitive work. In my opinion it should be encouraged in every organization, including the public service. After all, the man or woman on the job is usually more familiar with it than anyone in the background.

Another interesting and enlightened feature of the Leyland works was the practice of marking on the large machine tools the exact cost of the machine. The operator of a machine carrying a price of, say, £11,207, would treat it with due respect, as well as understanding further the importance of his job.

The shareholders' meetings were in those days always held at Leyland, and shareholders were given the opportunity afterwards of seeing over the works. Although the arrangement was often inconvenient from the point of view of travel, there is much to be said for holding meetings at the main place of operation. Shareholders are enabled to take a keener interest in their company, and employees are reminded that shareholders are real people who do exist.

During the first half of the 1960s, sporadic merger talks took place with BMC, and also with Jaguar, but as the yields on the shares of the three companies were so very disparate any idea of joining forces was extremely difficult. Then one day, to many people's great surprise, BMC joined forces with Jaguar, leaving Rover, apart from Rootes, the only independent motor manufacturer of any size. It was obvious to Leyland that it ought to acquire Rover, and perhaps more important that Rover should not join up with BMC.

After preliminary discussions between Black and George Farmer, the Rover chairman, Jock Backhouse (of Schroders), a non-executive director of Rover, and I were instructed to meet and endeavour to work out mutually agreeable terms. We knew each other well, and although we were on opposite sides of the fence, we were both familiar with the stock market and knew pretty well the right sort of price for Leyland to pay for Rover. After some pleasant bargaining and narrowing the difference to a minute figure, we split this small difference and reached agreement. Rover, alongside Standard-Triumph, fitted in very well with the Leyland group. It retained an acceptable measure of autonomy, though there was some heart-searching when their formerly enjoyed higher standard of living had to conform to the frugality of Leyland.

Those were the days of merger-mania. It was believed that the greater the size, the greater the efficiency and the higher the profitability. The mammoth GEC–AEI merger was on the horizon, and the phrase 'Small is beautiful' was not yet heard in business circles. So Leyland and BMH (as BMC had become after absorbing Jaguar) continued to eye each other from afar. But the courtship made no progress until a matchmaker appeared. This was no less than the Prime Minister of the day, Harold Wilson. And so a new compulsion was injected and both sides were on notice to talk to each other in serious vein. The talks started immediately. Stokes and I met Sir George Harriman, chairman of BMH, and John Pears, senior partner of Cooper Bros, auditors to BMH and a close financial adviser to BMH, in Stokes's flat in St James's Place. After a short exchange of views it was obvious that the ideas of the two companies were far apart, both in financial terms and in terms of structure of board and management.

In order to break the impending impasse I suggested that the largest shareholder common to both companies, the Prudential Assurance Company Ltd, should be consulted in confidence in the hope that it might suggest a mutually acceptable formula. This idea was accepted by both sides, and accordingly Pears and I called on the Prudential's investment chiefs, Gordon Clarke, Edward Hatchett and Peter Moody. After listening attentively to our tale they agreed to cooperate and awaited the next step, which was to receive the confidential estimates by each company of its prospects in the near future. They added, however, that as they had believed that BMH was in a recovery phase they

108

had been buying its shares for the past few weeks. Now that they had become privy to information about a possible merger they would stop buying.

When the Prudential men had received and digested the respective forecasts of the two companies and superimposed on them their own judgement of the future, they delivered their verdict. In a merged company BMH shareholders should receive 55 per cent of the equity and Leyland shareholders 45 per cent, though current market prices valued Leyland slightly more than BMH. It did not require any great effort or thought on my part to persuade my Leyland colleagues that such terms were wholly unacceptable, though we went through the motions of trying to get BMH to justify their forecasts, which were much more optimistic than Leyland were prepared to believe.

In the meantime Warburg's had been appointed advisers to Leyland, while BMH had appointed Schroder Wagg.

On 18 November 1967 the pound was devalued from $2.80 to $2.40 accompanied by fresh credit restrictions at home. This act was a benefit to Leyland with its large export and overseas business while it was a disadvantage to BMH, which depended greatly on a buoyant home market. The stock market recognized the changed conditions and the price of Leyland's 264 million shares of five shillings moved ahead of the price of BMH's 257 million shares of five shillings. Both sides began to realize that the only possible basis acceptable to both sides would be share-for-share.

This financial basis was the least difficult to resolve: the real difficulty was the corporate structure of the merged company and the part the leading hierarchy would play in it, in particular, Harriman, Stokes and Joe Edwards, who had become managing director of BMC. Many meetings took place, and in the latter stages Sir Frank Kearton (now Lord Kearton), chairman of the Industrial Reorganization Corporation (IRC), played an active and constructive part.

A full story of these discussions is given in Graham Turner's book *The Leyland Papers*.

Ultimately on 16 January 1968 agreement was reached and publicly announced whereby Leyland and BMH were to be merged on a share-for-share basis into the British Leyland Motor Corporation, with Sir George Harriman as chairman and Sir Donald Stokes as managing director. Each company appointed the same number of directors to the new company, and I was one of the Leyland appointees. The IRC was to provide a loan of £25 million.

The first step was to appoint about fifty study groups with equal membership from each side to examine every important aspect of the corporation's business. The merger was due to be approved by shareholders on 25 March to become effective on 13 May. In preparation, a 'dummy' board meeting was summoned for 12 February. There was a full turn-out: six from each side, with the secretary; the superstitious will note that this added up to thirteen. Almost everything that could have gone wrong went wrong, and it was the most unhappy meeting I have ever attended.

After the meeting, some of us moved to an adjoining room and were soon quizzing Ron Lucas, BMH's financial director, about BMH's current position and immediate outlook. We became so alarmed by what he said that we felt that everything must go back into the melting-pot. The Leyland directors, together with their adviser, Sir Sieg-mund Warburg, had urgent and critical meetings two days later and decided that in the light of the latest estimates from BMH they had no alternative but to call off the merger. I remember preparing a draft of a press release which, with some amendments, was approved by the Leyland board and communicated to BMH. I then went to a St Valentine's Day ball at the German Embassy, reflecting that it was a strange day to be taking part in a divorce before the parties had been properly married.

It is only fair to say that making a forecast of the profits of a high-volume motor manufacturer is a very chancy business – quite unlike a bus and truck business where nearly everything is 'made to order' and is much more predictable.

The principal mediators or advisers, Kearton, Warburg, Michael Verey (Schroder Wagg) and later the former Leyland chairman Lord Black were all determined to strive hard to prevent the 'divorce' going through. More than one midnight meeting was held, and a scheme was devised whereby Harriman would retire later in the year (to be appointed president) and Stokes would become chairman and managing director. After much searching of heart on both sides this was accepted and an exchange of letters confirming such intent was made. I thought at the time – and still do so – that the agreed change of chairman, within a few months, was a material fact which ought to have been disclosed to the shareholders, but the lawyers advised that it was not necessary.

The various meetings to ratify the merger were duly held and the resolutions passed. To my amazement, not a single question was asked at the Leyland meeting in Lancashire – there were only words of praise.

And so the British Leyland Motor Corporation, the second largest motor manufacturer outside the United States of America, set forth to justify itself and fulfil its founders' hopes. Its achievements and its troubles are public knowledge, and I will confine my concluding comments to a few particular aspects.

From the outset Donald Stokes, chairman and managing director, realized that it was wrong to combine these two offices in the same person. If he and his board could have agreed on who should be appointed managing director the appointment would no doubt have been made. But they could not agree, and so the idea remained only a desire. If it had been a compulsion then the best man available would have been appointed. There was no law of the land, nor even deep-rooted practice, to compel the separation of functions. It has a parallel in many ways with the efficiency of bicameral legislatures, whether it be Lords and Commons, or Senate and House of Representatives, with their inbuilt checks and counterbalances.

In time two deputy chairmen, Sir William Lyons and myself, were appointed. It was noted – and meant to be noted – that neither could be in the line of succession, if for no other reason than age. While there may be some exceptions, it is a good rule that in any big and important organization the heir-presumptives to the top jobs should be agreed and recognized even if only internally. This was one of the weaknesses of Leyland Motors before its merger with ACV.

During the time I was on the board of British Leyland there were two important moves which I endeavoured to initiate, but I failed in both. When I began to realize what an enormously complicated organization it was to manage – involving not just the merger of two companies, but the fact that each in turn had absorbed a number of subsidiaries, many of which were recently acquired – and the inevitable conflict between central control and local autonomy, I thought it would be advantageous to enlist the help of professional management consultants. I had recently attended a seminar organized by the British Institute of Management where the chief speaker had been Hugh Parker, the managing director of McKinsey & Co. (UK) Ltd. I was much impressed by what he said, especially about the role of the non-executive director. He pointed out that in the USA the ratio of non-executive to executive directors was about two to one, whereas in the UK it was the other way round. He added that the return on capital in the USA was about twice that in the UK. He did not imply that this difference was directly due to cause and effect, but he did not dispute that there was no connection.

I discussed the matter with my fellow non-executive

directors, who agreed with me, and I told Donald Stokes that I would like to propose at the next board meeting that management consultants should be appointed to examine and report. Unfortunately, at that meeting, because of illness or other reasons, I was the only non-executive director present and found myself in the minority of one, all the other directors being against the appointment. I accepted the decision in the frame of mind of one who had tried and failed – but I should not have left it at that. I should have insisted that the proposal be resubmitted at the next full board meeting, with the indication that I might resign if I were not satisfied. I do not know whether that would have altered the decision, but it would certainly have emphasized the importance I attached to it. Several years later, after I had retired from the board, Donald had the grace to admit that he wished he had agreed to the proposal; and I in turn pointed out the lack of support I got from our colleagues.

The second move was prompted by the observation that losses from the volume-car operations, Austin-Morris and Pressed Steel-Fisher, were in fact being staunched by profits from the truck and bus operations and the specialist car divisions. If British Leyland could be 'demerged' into these two parts then the loss-making (at the time) volume-car divisions would have to stand on their own feet with, in all probability, a salutary effect on labour relations. I prepared a paper demonstrating the feasibility, which involved splitting each BL share into two parts with an appropriate allocation of the corporation's debt. Not surprisingly, it was vehemently opposed by the executives, and that was that. I am still convinced that it might well have enabled part, at any rate, of BL to remain profitably in the private sector.

I tried as far as possible to visit many plants at home and overseas, usually on my own. This should normally be one of the duties of any director, and I found that nearly everyone in charge of local plants welcomed the opportunity of talking to a non-executive director. It was often easier to unburden their problems to someone outside the management hierarchy, and they usually appreciated the interest taken in what was often a lonely job.

The retiring age for all directors of BL was sixty-five and Bill Lyons and I bowed out at the AGM in the early spring of 1972. While 65 may be a proper age for retirement of executives bearing a heavy burden of active responsibility, it may be too early for part-time directors where age and experience may often add to their usefulness. I make no personal complaint. While, if requested, I would have stayed on, I was spared the trauma of seeing the corporation fall into the hands of the National Enterprise Board and public ownership.

My experience with the motor industry showed what could be done, and what could not be done, by a non-technical, non-executive director. Either alone, or in concert, much can be done to accelerate or add impetus to what would probably be done in any case. I found this to be so, with my colleague Herbert Hill, in the case of ACV. But against the determined opposition of the executive fraternity it is very difficult to succeed unless supported by most if not all of the non-executive directors or by unusually skilful advocacy.

At London and Manchester Assurance we successfully adopted a policy of having about one-half executive and one-half non-executive directors, and without a rigid application of this ratio I see no reason why that should not be the ideal for most companies, whether manufacturing or financial. A good team of non-executive directors should always ensure a good team of executives, for that is one of their primary tasks. But even a brilliant team of executives immersed, as they are in their day-to-day business, cannot always be relied on to enlist a competent team of non-executive directors.

CHAPTER 6

The Public Sector

Introduction Through Investment, 1945

My first introduction to the nationalized industries was in the spring of 1945, when I was working as investment manager of the Equity and Law Life Assurance Society. The Labour Party's manifesto gave prominence to its intention, if elected, to nationalize certain key sectors of the economy: the Bank of England, coal, rail transport, electricity, gas, iron and steel, cables and wireless. The 1945 election was in many ways unique. Because of the war, there had been no general election for ten years. Public opinion polls were still in their infancy and could give no confident forecast of the outcome. There was an interval of some three weeks between polling day and the declaration of the results in order to allow for the collection of votes by the armed forces still serving overseas.

Because of Winston Churchill's enormous prestige as a war leader, the Conservative Party expected to be returned – and most of the media took the same view. I remember thinking at the time that it was a wide-open contest. When the results were announced, the Stock Exchange, which shared the majority view of a Conservative Party victory, registered heavy falls, especially in the sectors threatened with nationalization.

At my first board meeting after the results I was asked

how the society was affected. I gave a summary of the holdings in the Bank of England, coal, electricity, gas, iron and steel, cables and wireless. A director then interjected and said that I had left out the railways. I was able to reply that we had none, but added that because of the new situation it might be right to buy. During the war the railways had been paid a fixed rental by the government but little if anything was known about their real earning power.

The basis of compensation for most nationalized undertakings was a formula based on recent market prices, to be satisfied in government guaranteed stock at its market value on vesting day. Coal, however, was the subject of arbitration, starting with a global sum which was then split into areas and then divided among the individual companies. Compensation for cables and wireless was also determined by arbitration before being allocated to the different classes of capital of the entitled companies. In all, there was considerable scope for intelligent guessing of the outcome of each security affected.

It was necessary therefore to study each bill as it was published and to follow its passage through Parliament. Each bill dealt with the particular requirements of the undertaking involved, but there was a common theme running through all of them: the obligation to balance income and expenditure, 'taking one year with another'. We all know now that such obligation has been honoured more in the breach than in the observance. As fair compensation was deemed to have been given and as each sector got the benefit of prime credit for its funding it was not thought at the outset that the financial obligation would be onerous. In the ensuing years governments frequently did much to prevent the nationalized boards from honouring their financial obligations, either by disallowing price increases or by frustrating the closing down of uneconomic enterprises, and little to encourage the observance.

In the several Nationalization Acts there is no sanction

against failure to make ends meet, nor has anyone been able to think of such a sanction at any time since. This must surely be an exceptional feature in the history of British legislation, and is one of the strongest indictments against the concept of public ownership.

National Coal Board, 1963–66

My next involvement with the public sector was in 1963 when I was invited to become a part-time member of the National Coal Board – the catalyst being my kind friend Nigel Birch. I was told that the Minister of Power wanted someone with financial and industrial experience, who need not have experience of coal, and who could give the necessary time. I was attracted by the idea, and accepted. I went through the preliminaries: first, an interview with the Minister, Richard Wood; secondly, instructions from the Ministry about what I must do and not do, that is, I must declare all my financial interests, and refrain from standing for Parliament, while a member of the board; thirdly, a meeting with the chairman, Lord Robens, and the deputy chairman Mr (later Sir) Humphrey Browne. I suggested to the chairman that it might be a good idea if I visited at an early date one of the best pits and one of the worst. He encouraged the former but discouraged the latter.

The full board met once a month, with all the senior officials, the meeting usually lasting about three hours or longer. Also once a month the National Advisory Council met, which comprised all board members and the chairmen of the territorial divisions. The paperwork was excellent, quite the best I have experienced in any organization in either the public or the private sector. Someone in the early days of the board must have set an example of good, simple English and efficient presentation. Every submission was preceded by a summary on one sheet of paper, followed by a full and detailed exposition. The statistical information was also of a very high standard: total output; output per man-shift; stocks, distributed and undistributed; absenteeism, voluntary and involuntary; profit and loss, etc.

I cannot pretend that part-time members had much opportunity to influence major decisions or policy, but each had the same vote as a full-time member. They had the right, if not the duty, to question and to persist until the question was fully answered; and perhaps most important of all they had the right of direct access, should occasion arise, to the Minister – and, indeed, I myself used this right on two occasions.

I duly visited one of the best pits, Ormonde Colliery, and spent a few hours underground. The pit was fully mechanized and automated. The coal was cut by machine, loaded and conveyed by conveyor belt, and the steel pit-props were moved by the press of a button. When they advanced they looked like the guards on parade lining up to 'dress by the right'. Decades ago, when all coal was hewn and loaded by hand, mining must always have been a very arduous job; but in the modern, highly mechanized and automated pits most of the strenuous effort has been eliminated, though much skill and labour is required in the installation and maintenance of the machinery.

Alas, I never visited one of the worst pits. I blame myself for the omission. I should have insisted, and I would not have been denied. It would be beneficial if everyone with responsibility, even if part-time, were to insist on seeing the worst of their organization. He may not be able to put things right on his own initiative, but pressures would be set in motion which would make the worst become less bad.

In October 1964 the Labour Party won the general election and Fred Lee became Minister of Power. The change of government had two significant consequences for the National Coal Board. First, the policy towards closures of pits was changed. Formerly they were handled on the merits of each case and with great skill and wisdom. When it became evident that a pit would have to be closed the local unions were informed and they usually accepted the decision. If there were any doubt a dialogue took place and differences of opinion were usually resolved. Preparations were made to offer redundant miners work in neighbouring pits, employment exchanges were alerted, and the information given to the board a few months after each closure usually showed that most if not all who were affected got new jobs.

When the government changed in 1964, the NCB was asked to classify each pit into one of three grades: A (good assured future); B (doubtful); or C (likely to close at an early date). While this classification was supposed to be top secret, it soon leaked out, which obviously made it more difficult to recruit in categories B and C, in addition to unsettling those who were already working there.

The second move was a capital reconstruction involving the writing-off of some £400 million of debt due to the Ministry. Although every board member was told the full facts and reasons I remember feeling unconvinced, though impotent to do much about it. As legislation was required, I went to the gallery of the House of Commons to listen to the second reading of the bill. It was a disappointing occasion. The House was poorly attended, with about thirty members on the government benches and even fewer on the opposition benches. The Minister opened with his prepared speech. Nearly all the interventions came from the mining MPs behind him, and few from the opposition. The shadow minister, John Peyton, did his best, but the result was a foregone conclusion. This was an important matter of principle, with which the Conservative opposition did not agree, and I felt it a pity that they did not issue a three-line whip and force the government to do likewise.

When my three-year term expired in 1966 I was invited to continue for another term, but I declined, partly because my other business commitments had increased but also because I was out of sympathy with some of the NCB's policy, in particular the lack of determination to carry out its financial obligations, and also the urge to expand production to an undue extent.

Transport Holding Company, 1971–73

My next involvement came in 1970 when the Conservatives won the general election. Towards the end of that year I was invited by the Minister of Transport, John Peyton, to take over the appointment of chairman of the Transport Holding Company. This state-owned company was the rump of a larger organization, and consisted mainly of travel activities, of which the largest was Thos. Cook & Son Ltd. While it was implied that these activities would be sold and the company wound up, no definite decision had been taken and new legislation would probably be needed. So at the outset I was involved in a company which had to be run as a continuing business.

I succeeded Sir Reginald Wilson, who remained chairman of Cooks. (The Minister thought it inappropriate to have the same person as chairman of both companies.) The directors of THC who continued to serve were Raymond Clifford-Turner, Sir Harry Crane, Hamish Falconer and B. H. Harbour. They were soon joined by Tom Grieve and Francis Perkins. They made a wise, efficient and cooperative team.

The two immediate problems related to Skyways Coach Air Ltd and Sir Henry Lunn Ltd (Lunn-Poly), both of which were losing money. The first was an ingenious idea of providing cheap travel between London and Paris. A coach was taken from London to Lympne, then a short air journey to Beauvais, followed by a coach to Paris. It provided a cheap journey for the passengers but unfortunately made no profit for the operator except from the sale of duty-free alcohol and tobacco. After several attempts to find a buyer which would take over the company as a going concern, we had unfortunately to appoint a receiver. The experienced firm of Cork, Gully & Co. took charge and made the best of a very difficult job. It was nearly two years before the last of the aeroplanes was sold.

Lunn-Poly was essentially a 'package-tour' firm. This involved contracting for seats in aeroplanes, and for hotel beds. Ideally, these should balance, and if they did, and were occupied to near-capacity, then big profits could be expected. But the ideal never happened. When the numbers of aeroplane seats and the numbers of beds became unbalanced the deficiency was always made good by contracting for more of the lesser one, never by disposing of the surplus. Whether or not Transport Holding Company continued in business, this was a 'loss-maker' which would be better sold, and the only hope was to find someone who believed it could be turned into a 'profit-maker'. There were not many candidates. In the end, the company was sold to a travel subsidiary of Cunard Steamship Company Ltd, although not long afterwards it was sold on to Thomson Holidays.

I learned at an early date that the only safe way of making money in the travel business is to act as an agent for other firms' tours, and seldom, if ever, to act as a principal.

Cooks, during the 'continuing business' period, gave little cause for anxiety. It had its own board and management. Being a firm believer in the merits of the part-time director, I encouraged the appointment to the board of Cooks of Stanley Field, chairman of William Baird & Co. Ltd, and Bill Morrison, a partner in Thomson McLintock & Co., chartered accountants. The inhibitions of public ownership, however, were seldom absent. Cooks could not open a new branch of any significance without the consent, through THC, of the Minister. Also, no wage settlement could be implemented without similar consent.

Plans were soon in progress to dispose of Cooks. John Peyton had convinced the Cabinet that it should be sold to the private sector. Although there was an element of doubt whether legislation would be needed, a bill was introduced to provide for the disposal of assets of THC and its dissolution. Provision was also made for pensions and compensation for loss of office in respect of employees of bodies which ceased to be subsidiaries of the company. The bill was introduced in the late autumn of 1971 and received the Royal Assent in March 1972.

I went to the gallery of the House of Commons to listen to the second reading. The debate followed party policy and the outcome was predictable, but the afternoon was far from unexciting. It was the day when a large-scale demonstration by the unemployed outside the House of Parliament took place. During the course of the debate some member raised a point of order from the Bar of the House, asking if Mr Speaker were aware of what was going on outside, adding: 'The mounted police have lost control.' The front benches and the press gallery filled rapidly and the Leader of the House, William Whitelaw, rose to propose that, as no one in the House knew what was going on outside, the chief whips of both the government and the opposition should go out and report their findings. This was agreed, and soon afterward they returned to report that over a hundred 'strangers' were inside the Palace of Westminster, and that about the same number were trying to get in, adding: 'We let them in.' The undramatic debate resumed, soon to meet with another intervention. A member complained that he had been forcibly prevented by the police from meeting one of his constituents. It later transpired that this was because the police had been reinforced by many who, unlike the police usually on duty, did not recognize all the members. The crisis was defused as quickly as it had blown up. I thought afterwards that I had witnessed the 'Mother of Parliaments' at its best, quietly, efficiently and effectively dealing with a sudden emergency.

In anticipation of the necessary legislation, plans were set in motion to offer Cooks for sale. The first step was to appoint a merchant bank, and J. Henry Schroder Wagg & Co. Ltd was chosen for the purpose. It proved to have been a very wise choice, and they carried out their work with great skill. It is only fair to add that many other merchant banks would also have made a good job of it, though each in a different way, but there are many advantages in a matter of such complexity of knowing well the people involved, as I and several of my colleagues did; also the Minister was very happy with the choice. The people assigned to the task by Schroders were: Hugh Ashton, Sir Henry Fisher, Ben Strickland, and Simon Richardson, and to each and all I remain deeply grateful.

A prospectus was compiled and comprised no less than forty-four pages. The arrangements for sale had to be specially designed for this unique operation. Since the Minister, who had become part of the Department of the Environment, would have to give consent to the purchase, each applicant was required to submit a memorandum outlining how, if successful, he would operate Cooks. The applicant was allowed to ask questions, the replies to which would be sent to all prospective purchasers. The THC would compile a short-list of applicants (with the approval of the Minister) and these short-listed applicants would be interviewed by the THC. They would then be given one chance – and one only – to increase the sum offered, which would then become unconditional.

There was no precedent for an operation of this nature. The rules had to be made *ab initio*, by the THC and its advisers, with the consent of the Minister. There were many possible variations, but with the benefit of hindsight I do not think any major change would have been made: indeed, I like to think that the rules we adopted could serve as a pattern for any similar operation in the future.

Two applicants qualified for the short-list: the Barclays Bank syndicate, and the Midland Bank syndicate. When the time came for the interviews some of my colleagues suggested that all the members of the THC board should be present; but in a matter like this it would have been impossible to rehearse and control all the answers to the questions, so it was decided to leave it to the chairman, supported by his advisers. They were difficult meetings for both sides. Each contestant tried hard to find out what his opponent had bid, and I formed the opinion that each was even more determined to prevent his opponent from succeeding than to win himself. This was understandable. Each side exercised its right to increase its offer, and the Midland Bank/ Trust House Forte/Automobile Association syndicate won with a figure of £22,500,000, which in financial jargon was an exit price/earnings ratio of 46. The price was far higher than anyone had hoped for at the outset, but one glittering prize was the float of unpresented travellers' cheques which shortly before the offer for sale had exceeded £25 million and for the previous three years had never been less than £12 million. Such is the lethargy and inertia of travel customers.

When soon afterwards a celebration meeting was held at the Department of the Environment, in an atmosphere of euphoria I suggested that the THC team and advisers were ready to help with the next task of denationalization and cited the group of transport hotels as a suitable candidate. I had in mind the interest which some of the leading hotel chains would show and the premium they might pay to outbid their competitors. I was discouraged by the observation that there were more urgent priorities. I still think that private capital should replace public capital in this field. It is conceded that the management is good, but much of the original *raison d'être* has gone; for example, the Gleneagles, Turnberry and St Andrew's hotels are now all far distant from their nearest railheads. In 1983 most of these hotels were being advertised for sale.

124

The final accounts of the Transport Holding Company gave a summary of its results from 1 January 1963 to 31 March 1973. They showed consolidated trading profits over the period of £90,300,000 with profits, less losses, on the realization of travel and tourism assets of £12,900,000. The trading profits arose mainly from road haulage and bus companies in the earlier years, before they were transferred to the National Freight Corporation, the National Bus Company and the Scottish Transport Group.

It is a sad thought that it was one of the most profitable state enterprises that was terminated. Its success was due to several factors. Its operations were competitive and not monopolistic. It had a small central staff led in its early days by a very competent chairman, the late Sir Philip Warter. It was capable of making profits and expected to make them: the subsidy of losses was never necessary. It did not prove the case for state ownership, but showed what resilience and determination of good management could do.

National Freight Corporation, 1971–74

As my work with the THC was coming to its end I was invited by John Peyton to join the board of the National Freight Corporation, and I accepted. This was housed in the same building, Argosy House, Great Portland Street, and it shared many of its staff with the THC. Its board consisted of D. E. A. Petitt, now Sir Daniel Petitt, as chairman, and about ten part-time members. It was a holding company whose main operating subsidiaries were British Road Services, National Carriers, Freightliners and Pickfords, each with its own chief executive responsible to the NFC board. None had any monopoly or captive customers, so the keen wind of competition was a constant drive towards economy and efficiency.

The board met once a month, for three hours. Every few months the chief executive of the operating companies presented his report, outlined his policy and invited questions. The paperwork, information and statistical service and financial returns were all excellent, and every member of the board knew well what was 'going on'. He knew enough about the senior management to form an informed opinion when promotions or change or duties were put forward for consideration. Every year a visit was made by the board to one of the main provincial centres where several of the more important customers were entertained, after which useful discussions were held.

During most of my three-year term reasonable profits were made – and were expected to be made – but near the end of my time the red ink started to appear. Instead of a compulsion to make ends meet, the insidious disease of the public sector began to appear: any deficit would be made good by public subsidy. I could not stay long enough to fight a rearguard action.

Conclusion

My involvement with the public sector terminated in 1974, and I can sum up my experience as follows. I found that the day-to-day management and administration could be just as good as in the private sector, and was sometimes even better. This is no doubt due to people in responsible positions doing their best whatever the nature of their business. Efficiency and profitability are best when the organization is making a profit. When this happens there is an urge to maximize profits and not to be content with a minimum level. But when losses are the order of the day the tendency is to look to government to make good the losses by various methods of subvention. There is not the compelling urge, as in the private sector, to do everything possible to make ends meet.

I have frequently asked my friends the hypothetical question of what would have happened if the British railways had not been nationalized. The quick reply has usually been that they would have gone bankrupt. I then direct thought to the American railroads, which have faced similar difficulties to the British and have mostly survived; indeed some have reached a higher level of profitability – because the compulsion was there. For example, New York Central Railroad encouraged the building of high-rise office blocks above Grand Central Station in New York to the benefit of all concerned, not least the commuting public. But where are similar developments, potentially just as beneficial, above, say, Victoria Station or Liverpool Street Station? No doubt British Rail has tried, and may try again, but the compulsion under private enterprise would have been much more determined.

I remain convinced that nationalization has been one of the most debilitating events in Britain's post-war history, and I wish fervently that any 'non-left' government would make a much more determined attempt to reverse the process. Obviously, some (coal, electricity, gas, railways) are beyond recall; though some of their peripheral activities, such as hotels, are not. But candidates for return to the private sector include: National Freight Corporation, already agreed and implemented; British Leyland, or parts of it; British Airways, British Aerospace; British Transport Docks; Cable & Wireless; and the telephone service; a study might even be made of a feasibility of dealing with the Bank of England, where the move to public ownership started first in 1945.

POSTSCRIPT:
Past Regrets
and Future Hopes

Most people having had a full and varied business life retain some regrets of the past and hopes for the future, and I am no exception. On reflection, there are many things I would have done differently, and one in particular stands out: the part I played in the merger between Leyland and BMH. With the benefit of hindsight, and perhaps if I had used wiser judgement at the time, I feel that I should have done my utmost to oppose the merger instead of encouraging it.

If the merger had not taken place, and the two companies had remained separate, the Leyland Motor Corporation would in all probability have continued to prosper and would have remained profitable today – outside the public sector. BMH would have been under compulsion to live and fight on its own, and even if it came under the wings of the NEB and public ownership, that would have been a part only of what is now BL. I remember at the time of the merger being asked a direct question by the sponsoring Minister, Anthony Wedgwood Benn, Minister of Technology. 'If this merger had not come off, what would have happened to BMH?' I replied that the largest institutional shareholder, believed to be the Prudential Assurance Company, would probably have gone in private to the chairman and managing director, disclosed their worries and discussed ways and means of improving matters. He did not dissent, and I truly believe that such pressures would have borne fruit.

But one still has to form a judgement at the time, without the benefit of hindsight. I entered the negotiations with conviction, having been instructed that bigger would be better but without any explanation of why that should be so. When agreement had been reached and Leyland had decided subsequently to withdraw, I felt disappointed, yet with an inward peace that a right decision had been taken. In supporting the resuscitation I was, I think, more influenced by the potential good to the British motor industry and to the country as a whole than by any benefit to Leyland shareholders. If I had thought only about the effect on Leyland shareholders I might have acted differently – I don't know – but I should certainly have been more aware that my first loyalty was to them. I erred in trying to serve two masters. I was paid by Leyland to serve their interests. But while this regret related to action over a decade ago there is still the future; and what do I think now are the best hopes for BL's future?

Being a convinced believer in private enterprise, I fervently hope that British Leyland can be bought out of the public sector. I see no hope of this happening in its present form. Some form of 'demerging' would be necessary first. There is a reasonable hope that the truck and bus divisions and the specialist car divisions – Jaguar, Rover, Triumph – could be sold on satisfactory terms by a prospectus to the private investor. The volume-car divisions, Austin-Morris, and the related body plants, Pressed Steel-Fisher, with their volatile turnover and profit and loss accounts, would be a much more difficult matter. The only organizations likely to be interested would be the multinational car firms such as Citroën, Ford, General Motors, Volkswagen, and possibly Nissan or Toyota. While the profit record of the BL volume-car divisions in recent years is uninspiring, large facilities and capacity could be offered on

129

terms materially lower than the cost of building similar new capacity. If no multinational were very keen to acquire such an investment for itself, each potential candidate would no doubt be most reluctant to see any of its competitors succeed. So the possibility may not be entirely hopeless, and it should be worth a try. Such then are my hopes for BL in the early 1980s.

During my years with the motor industry I was able to observe the course of industrial relations, though was never directly involved in negotiations between management and union. I recollect, about two or three years after the formation of British Leyland, Donald Stokes saying one day to his colleagues: 'This is a red-letter day. We haven't a stoppage in a plant anywhere in the organization.' Although strikes and go-slows were all too frequent, much good work was done by both sides to improve production; but they were up against a structural disadvantage, which was the multiplicity of craft unions. There is no such organization as a British motor union.

The Economist of 2 June 1979 reported in full Sir Nicholas Henderson's valedictory despatch to the Foreign Secretary at the time, David Owen, on his transfer of ambassadorship from Paris to Washington. The despatch compared the industrial performances of Britain, France and West Germany, which were far from flattering to Britain. He pointed out that neither Germany nor France had craft unions, membership being based not on occupation but on the industry in which the person works. In West Germany there were 17 fully integrated industrial unions, compared with 115 trade unions affiliated to the TUC in Britain. (And it was Britain which was mainly responsible for instructing West Germany how to re-establish trade unions after the Second World War!)

I was so impressed by the arguments in this despatch that in an endeavour to get the ball rolling further I wrote a letter, which was published in *The Times*, inviting discussion on the subject of trade union structure. The response was nil. The replacement of craft unions by industrial unions cannot be done by legislation. It will need an enlightened decision by the unions themselves. Apart from the practical and organizational difficulties, the vested interests against change may be powerful. I firmly believe that the restructuring of unions in Britain into industrial unions would do more for productivity and improved industrial relations than any amount of legislation. Another beneficial move would be greater encouragement of the secret ballot. No one should be against this in principle: for example, by its own constitution the National Union of Mineworkers cannot call a strike without a secret ballot.

So, high among my hopes for the future of the industry are industrial unions and secret ballots. They will surely come in time; but why not sooner rather than later?

Another debilitating factor in British life is the subsidy, though it is less so now than formerly. The most deeprooted of these is housing by local authorities. There are two major adverse effects. First is the immobility of labour: tenants of council houses who become unemployed are reluctant to move into an area where employment prospects are better unless they can get another subsidized house. At the time of writing the idea is being mooted that a small percentage of council houses should be reserved for people coming into the community from another locality, in search of work. The second adverse effect is that the resulting increase in local rates can have a devastating effect on local businesses; witness the driving out of the once famous large shops in Sauchiehall Street, Glasgow, where housing subsidies are among the highest in the land.

What is needed and desirable, in addition to allowing council-house tenants to buy their houses, is the encouragement of private building of houses to let, with little or no rent control. The ideal would be a supply of dwellings rather greater than the demand; as used to happen most of the time in the inter-war years. This may sound like a pipe-dream, but there is one practical measure which government could take to facilitate the withdrawal or reduction of subsidies. I refer to the system of negative income tax or tax credit. This would mean in effect that everyone would have to make a return of income: those above a certain level would pay taxes; those below would receive a subvention from the state. Mr Heath's government issued a green paper on the subject. It has the purpose of a means-test without any of the stigma, and I hope this enlightened idea will be brought up to date and enacted.

I think there is almost universal agreement that the ideal system of social security is to help only those in genuine need, through no fault of their own. The only practical method is to ensure that everyone makes a return of income. If this were to be enacted I hope that by skilful questioning a proper declaration would be made of the so-called 'black economy'. No one knows for certain, though a recent estimate was given officially in the House of Commons that the loss of tax revenue was as high as £4,000 million. The present system seems inadequate to cope with it.

I wish I knew a simple answer to, or remedy for, inflation. But there can be little doubt that it is the most serious threat to our modern economy. There is some emphasis at present on increasing the supply of goods and services – the so-called 'supply-side' theory. Increasing the supply can be just as effective on prices as decreasing the demand, as well as being more satisfying. Of course the encouragement of saving is a useful antidote, and the more attractive the form of saving the greater the stimulus. At the time of writing the government is enlarging the scope of 'granny' bonds, but I hope it will persevere with the issue, without any restrictions, of index-linked government stock with a low fixed coupon, say 2½ per cent. Restriction to pension funds is not good enough.

In the event of great success and the reduction of inflation to low single figures – with a substantial fall in interest rates – it would be just and equitable to offer holders of index-linked stocks with the right of conversion into a conventional non-indexed stock with a fixed rate of interest, for example, 9 per cent, which might well in such circumstances be above the market rate ruling at the time of conversion.

As institutional investment has been one of my main activities, there are naturally a few things I would still like to see done. I hope the present qualified intentions to remove the ban on all companies' being allowed to buy, and later if desired reissue their own shares, will be made good and applied to all companies. This facility has, I think, been of great benefit to the American economy, without any noticeable abuses.

While it is the practice of most company pension funds to forbid the purchase of the company's own shares, I hope it will soon be legally banned. I had a practical experience of this when I was serving on a panel of advisers to the Rolls-Royce pension fund. I noticed that the fund had a modest holding of Rolls-Royce ordinary shares, which at the time was one of the leading 'blue chips' and a constituent of the FT 30-share index. I persuaded my colleagues that this was wrong in principle, though unlikely to be vulnerable in practice. It proved in time to be also wrong in practice. I believe in the funding of private sector company pension funds, and think it is sounder for the public sector to do likewise rather than 'pay as you go'. Pension funds are such an enormous and increasing factor in investment markets that their control and administration is vitally important. Without criticizing the present practice, I hope the counter-part of the non-executive director can be injected more frequently into the role of independent trustee. Usually trustees of pension funds are confined to members or ex-members of the employing organization. I hope there will be a greater leavening of outside expertise.

I look forward with hope to a much more determined effort to privatize the public sector. Some candidates are on the near horizon.

It is sad to contemplate at the time of writing the closure of some British Steel Corporation plants, in particular Corby, once the pride of the former Stewarts and Lloyds Ltd, and Shotton, once the pride of the former John Summers & Co. Ltd. It would be wonderful if some private enterprises could make a successful bid. Any price in excess of the scrap value, less the cost of redundancy payments, should be beneficial to BSC. The buyer would acquire a much relieved and willing labour force, would gain the profound goodwill of the local community, and should be immune from future threats of renationalization. This may be a very remote hope, but 'long odds-against' chances do sometimes happen.

I have already expressed my profound belief that in most commercial undertakings private enterprise is better than public ownership. This belief can be supported by a case history of a recent privatization. I have chosen National Freight Corporation, which was bought out of public ownership in February 1982, largely because its fortunes before and after this event can be satisfactorily examined. The transfer of ownership was a 'buy-out' by the managers and staff, the new company being named the National Freight Consortium PLC. The price paid to the government was £53,500,000, though the greater part of this was paid over to the pension funds' trustees to extinguish a heavy deficiency. The NFC borrowed a medium-term loan from its bankers of £51 million, and the ordinary capital was £7,500,000. £6,200,000 of ordinary capital was offered to employees, and was oversubscribed.

It might be possible to compare the financial results shortly before the 'buy-out' with those soon afterwards, but there are so many extraneous factors that a true comparison would be difficult. A better measure of the fortunes is to be found in the 'fair price' of the shares. Since there is no Stock Exchange quotation, an independent firm of accountants periodically establishes the transfer price. This price, adjusted to allow for a bonus issue of one share for each share held in April 1983, is as follows:

Date	February 1982	August 1982	October 1982	March 1983	May 1983	August 1983
	£	£	£	£	£	£
Price	1.00	1.65	2.00	2.45	3.20 (1.60)	3.40 (1.70)

The fair price must obviously reflect the current balance sheet, current trading and future prospects and is, therefore, as good an indication as can be found of the company's fortunes. A noteworthy feature of the new company is the interest shown by the employee-shareholders. Quarterly regional meetings are held with directors, with questions and answers. At the first annual general meeting held in Birmingham in February 1983, no fewer than 1,700 share-holders attended – which puts to shame the attendance at the AGMs of most British companies.

The success of the NFC, under the able chairmanship of Sir Peter Thompson, is an argument not only for privatiz-ation but also for employee-shareownership. In various ways this is being encouraged by many British companies. There is no need to advance additional arguments for the benefit of employee-shareownership, except perhaps to note the similarity with home ownership: a householder owning his own home is likely to look after it much better than if it is rented, especially if from a public authority.

To close on a hopeful note, I cannot do better than quote another couplet from Tennyson's 'Locksley Hall':

Men, my brothers, men the workers, ever reaping something new:
That which they have done but earnest of the things that they shall do.

Index

140

141

This book is to be returned on or before
the last date stamped below.

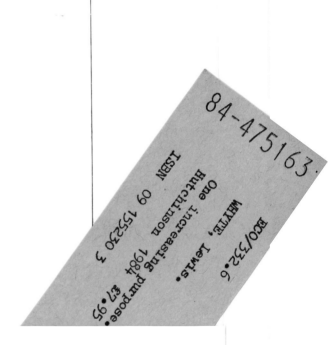

SURREY COUNTY LIBRARY

(Headquarters, West Street, Dorking)

This book must be returned to the Branch or
Travelling Library from which it was borrowed, by the
latest date entered above.

Charges will be payable on books kept overdue.

L.22